SANGRIA
Recipes

Lisa Shea

wineintro.com

Copyright

Dedication

To Bob
for supporting my wine writing efforts
for over fifteen years -
thank you for everything!

Table of Contents

Introduction

Sangria recipes are the inspiration for many red wine punch styles. *Sangria* as a named drink was created in Spain and made popular in the US at the 1964 World's Fair. It normally has red wine, brandy, and fruit. However, it can be made in just about any style you can imagine.

Sangria as a mixture did not spring from the ether in the 1960s - or even in the 1800s. Rather, the idea of mixing wine, alcohol and fruit has been around for many centuries. For most European parties this concoction was the center of attention - a big bowl full of fruit and wine that people would ladle into cups or glasses.

The beauty of sangria is that you can make it to perfectly match the event. You can use oranges, lemon and citrus fruit to give freshness to a hot day. You can create a dense blend of blueberries and blackberries to warm you up at a wintry celebration.

It's no surprise that in modern times Sangria is the perfect party punch that just about everybody loves! Fresh, fruity, delicious, Sangria can be made in any number of styles from spicy to mild to rich to bubbly. You can make sangria with red wine, white wine, and even sparkling wine. The sparkling wine from Spain is known as *cava*.

Read on below to find the perfect Sangria recipe to meet your party needs!

Sangria Recipes

A History of Sangria

From its humble roots in Spain, Sangria has grown to become a popular, refreshing party drink around the world. In the United States, Sangria was first tasted at the 1964 World's Fair in New York. The Spanish World area served this fruity wine punch to its visitors, and history was made!

Sangria is based on the traditional red wine punch popular across Europe for hundreds of years. The punch base would be *claret*. Claret is the British term for Bordeaux wine from Bordeaux, France. This red wine is traditionally made from a blend of cabernet sauvignon, cabernet franc and merlot. Brandy and fruit would be added to the red wine punch for flavor. In the 1700s and 1800s, Claret Cup Punch could be found at parties of all sizes. This would be the drink of choice for Jane Austen heroines, for example.

Going back even further in time, *hippocras* is a well-documented drink concoction enjoyed in the middle ages. This was traditionally a wine with various spices added in - ginger, cinnamon, and so on.

Why the emphasis on wine? Remember that until modern times water was often unsafe to drink. People would bathe in it, wash their horses in it, and so on. Milk was considered a "baby food" only. That meant - even for toddlers - that the only safe liquid to drink had at least some alcohol in it. The alcohol would take care of any bacteria in the drink. Most households made some wine from fruits and berries in the area. It was very natural to "liven things up" by adding more spices, fruits, and other items to the wine to give it a different flavor.

Looking more specifically at Spain, this region was actively planted with vineyards by the Romans when they swept through about 200BC. A very active wine shipping trade promptly began, with the beautiful wines of Spain supplying much of Rome's drinking desires. Red grapes grew very well here and have been enjoyed ever since. The locals named their wine punches, in all their varieties, as *Sangria*.

Sangria is traditionally a red wine punch. Spanish people from all walks of life enjoy this drink, creating it primarily with Rioja and other Spanish reds. Sangria can also be made with white wine. With white wine the sangria is then known as 'Sangria Blanco' (white sangria). The Cava (Spanish sparkling wine) producing area soon created a sparkling white version.

In the south of Spain Sangria is often called *zurra*. This version of sangria is created with peach or nectarine.

Sangria is typically created from red wine, fruit juices, soda water, fruit and sometimes brandy. When making your own Sangria, use a good quality wine, and if at all possible let it chill overnight. This lets the fruit flavors blend into the drink. If you can, use Rioja to get the authentic Spanish flavor, but definitely choose something you like - you're the one drinking it! In the morning, pour your sangria into a pitcher full of ice cubes, garnish with fresh fruit, and enjoy.

Every restaurant has its own sangria recipe - typically a mix of wine, brandy and fresh fruits, served over ice. It's one of the most individualistic drinks on the market. Don't just buy a mix at the store - have fun and create your own! Sangria's appeal is all about taking your favorite wine, your favorite fruits, and experimenting with them.

Sangria Recipes

How to make Sangria

Luckily for wine drinkers everywhere, sangria is not a mysterious concoction that requires exotic ingredients or bizarre cooking traditions. Making sangria is not making a creme brulee, requiring you to carefully brown and caramelize sugar. Rather, sangria is a casual, fun party punch that countless Spaniards have been making in their back yards for centuries. The key words for sangria making are fun, fun, and more fun. :)

To start with, sangria involves wine. So you do need a bottle of wine - or at least a glass of it! Sangria can be made on small or large scales. For the sake of this discussion let's assume you have a 750ml or larger bottle of wine that you want to turn into sangria, either to enjoy on your own or to share with friends at a party.

You need to find something to put this wine into, to serve. Traditionally this would be a ceramic pitcher. Other partiers would get one of those large punch bowls with a ladle so that people could serve out their own sangria easily without having to lift up a heavy pitcher. Either one works. In a pinch you can always use a large cooking pot and a regular old soup ladle.

OK, pour in the wine. Note that it can be red, white, rose, bubbly or anything else you find. Sangria is about enjoying yourself and exploring your options.

Step one is complete!

Now comes the making sangria part. You want to add things to this wine to liven it up. Traditionally people would simply go wandering into their back yards and see what was in season. Are the blueberries ripe? Are the oranges round and luscious? If you have a back yard garden, this could be the perfect time to harvest! If you visit a store, you probably have even more options open to you. So add in a few of your favorites. Orange wheels. Strawberries, some cut up, some whole. Peach pieces. Kiwi! Your imagination is the limit. Remember that when people are pouring or ladling that they'll either be seeking to grab some of these pieces or avoid them. Small pieces are fun to "drink down" and enjoy with the liquid - but larger pieces might be choking hazards. Plan appropriately :) Having a whole strawberry, for example, adds visual appeal and is also easy to grab with the fingers. This means the sangria fan not only gets to drink their sangria but also to nibble on a whole sangria-soaked strawberry at the same time.

Sangria also involves liquor. You can add in some brandy or vodka for no-extra-flavor kick, or you can go for Grand Marnier, Triple Sec, Peach Schnapps or the many other flavored liqueurs to get some added flavor. It's all up to you and what end result you're aiming for.

In the ideal world this whole concoction would sit overnight to really soak. That way the fruit flavors get absorbed by the liquid and vice versa. Also, you normally want to drink this cold. If you are in a rush, dump in some ice cubes - or even better buy some frozen fruit and berries. That way they serve as natural ice cubes and also add flavor as they "melt" rather than diluting your mixture.

For serving, sangria is about casual fun. Go with sturdy glasses rather than delicate thin glassware. You don't want to be dancing around shards of glass after one or two glasses are consumed! If you look at Spanish restaurant photos you'll see they tend to use very thick sturdy water type glasses for Sangria. Sangria is all about enjoying yourself and relaxing.

Have fun with your sangria creations, and good luck making sangria!

Sangria Recipes

Sangria FAQs

Sangria is a delicious wine punch traditionally made with wine and brandy. Here are some frequently asked questions about sangria!

Does Sangria Need to be Refrigerated?

Sangria does have some alcohol in it, so it isn't likely to become "poisonous". However, Sangria has wine and fruit in it - and these things tend to decay in warmth. Wine becomes vinegar rather quickly once exposed to air. Fruit of course gets mushy and falls apart. It's really in your best interest to keep your Sangria in the fridge at all times - and use ice cubes when it's out on the table. For the ice cubes, you can either use real ones or plastic ones which won't melt and dilute your punch.

How Long will Sangria Last?

The base of sangria is wine. Wine, once you expose it to air, quickly tastes sour like vinegar. In a bottle, you at least have the container sealed so that the volume of air touching the sangria is relatively small, and it can last a few days to a week. With sangria, you usually have it in a wide mouthed pitcher. I would drink this in a day or two before the vinegar flavors become too strong. It's not that the sangria will become "poisonous" in that period of time - but drinking vinegar is not usually a tasty pastime.

Is Sangria Always Red?

It's true that many restaurants assume the word sangria means a red wine blend. However, sangria can be made with white wine or sparkling wine as well. It's completely up to you! Start with a wine you enjoy, add in your favorite fruits and berries, and top it off with a bit of liquor. Enjoy!

What does the word "Sangria" mean?

The Spanish language is a fascinating one - I studied it for six years! My father and stepmother both speak Spanish fluently, as my father spent some of his childhood in Brazil. It is a lovely language full of nuance.

Sangria Recipes

The root word in Spanish is "sangre" which means "blood". However, you can be even more specific. The word in Spanish for "bleeding" is actually "sangria". The connection here is not of course that sangria has blood in it :) Rather, it is that the rich, red color of blood matches the vibrant hue of the sangria drink. In many cultures blood was the symbol of life, of vitality, of a full experience and passion. This is what sangria embodies!

What is the One Authentic Sangria Recipe?

This is sort of like asking what the one authentic chicken recipe is in the United States. There are literally thousands of chicken recipes, and all of them are completely authentic. Some use garlic. Some use dill. Some use a grill, some use a stove. Each one is delicious in its own way.

The same is absolutely true for sangria. Remember, sangria didn't "spring into existence" in Spain in the 1900s. People had been making red wine punches in Europe for hundreds of years. Claret Cup was a staple at fancy parties and cottage gatherings alike. People grabbed whatever wine was handy (red, white, or otherwise), whatever fruit was in their back yard, and tossed in some hard alcohol. Voila! They had a drink.

If you go to 100 different towns in Spain you'll find 100 different traditional recipes. That is the beauty of sangria. It is adaptable, delicious, and takes full advantage of whatever is in season at the moment. It is the ultimate flexible beverage.

What Traditional Pitcher is Used for Sangria?

The image shown below of a pitcher is the traditional pitcher for Sangria, created in Spain especially for the purpose of serving sangria.

The pinched lip at the front of the pitcher helps to catch the fruit in the sangria and keep it from cascading down into the person's glass! The ceramic container helps to keep the sangria cool on a hot summer's day.

Sangria Recipes

What Is the Best Wine for Sangria?

I get this question every once in a while, from avid Sangria drinkers. What is the best wine for Sangria? This is sort of like asking what the best cheese is for eating, or what the best ice cream flavor is for kids.

The thing is that every one of us has different taste buds. A cabernet that I adore for being light and fruity, you might hate for being dry and dusty. We really do taste things differently. If someone is raised on soda and sweets they might find a typical chardonnay to be way too dry. Another person who was raised on drinking water and eating melba toast might find that exact same chardonnay to be way too sweet and buttery.

Sangria is a very wide open punch style that can involve red wines, white wines, sparkling wines. Sangria can be made with liquors of every shape and style - rums, vodkas, brandies, melon flavors, strawberry flavors. You can make sangria with strawberries. Sangria with peaches. Sangria with plums. You can see how wildly the flavors can vary!

So in terms of wines, it then makes sense that the wines that would match up - even in a general sense - would also vary wildly. If you made a white wine sangria with peaches and ginger ale, you might want a light riesling along with asti spumanti. If you made a heavy red wine sangria with strawberries, black cherries, raspberries and Grand Marnier you might go with a rich cabernet.

Even with a given fruit combination there is no absolute "must have" wine. You could do peaches and ginger ale and go with prosecco and ice wine for a super sweet, confectioner's sugar style sangria. You could do peaches and ginger ale with chardonnay and have a more buttery, rich experience. All are equally valid and equally delicious for most people. I'm sure you could also find people who would hate these as being "too sweet"! That's the way taste buds are.

The fun of sangria is that there are so many options. You go with what *you* love. If you personally love strawberries, start there. Get a container of strawberries, some friends, and three or four of your favorite red wines. Now sit around for an afternoon sampling wines and strawberries. Which do you love together?

Sangria Recipes

Which don't work out well? Once you know what *your* taste buds find pleasing, you can play with sangria mixes, adding in liqueurs and sodas until the flavor combination is just right!

Sangria Recipes

Sangria and Appetizers

OK, so you've got your Sangria mixed and prepared for serving. Now the big question - what goes best with your delicious sangria? Fear not! We've got some delicious options for you here.

Pepperjack Cheese
Yup, for a cheese, my prime choice would be pepperjack. You want something strong and flavorful to stand up to the rich flavor of the Sangria. Serve on something hefty, like a Triscuit.

Sheep Cheese
Spain is famous for its sheep, which roam the native Spanish landscape with great dexterity. Sheep-milk based cheese are loved throughout Spain. Manchego and Roncal are two styles you can look for to bring an authentic Spanish flavor to your evening.

Calamari
This is after all a Spanish punch, so all of those Spanish dishes work very well here. Fried calamari works great for the seafood-loving nation, is are easy to eat!

Fried Shrimp
See the previous comment. :) Shrimp are well loved by most people, and goes perfectly with the punch.

Spicy Meatballs
Grab some fancy toothpicks and lay out a platter or two of delicious meatballs. What could be better?

Sangria Recipes

Sangria Ingredients

Sangria is a traditional Spanish alcoholic drink that is loved around the world. Here are the ingredients to have on hand so you're always ready to create a Sangria Recipe that's adored!

Wine

Sangria always involves wine. While many people enjoy a red wine sangria, there are also white wine sangrias and sparkling wine sangrias. Whatever wine you love, a sangria can be made out of it. Now, granted, some types of wine tend to taste better with fruit than others. Mix and match until you find which are perfect for your taste buds! Some people favor sweeter wines, some prefer dryer wines. It is completely up to you.

Liqueur

One aspect of sangria is that it is a fruity wine with a kick. There is almost always a hard alcohol component to a sangria. This can be something "straight" like rum, gin or vodka. It can also be something that adds flavor, like Grand Marnier (orange flavored) or Midori (melon flavored). Fruit flavored liqueurs work really well with sangria. Keep a few of these on your shelves.

Fruit / Berries

I know, fresh fruit goes bad really quickly. Berries can be even worse. It's a struggle for me to eat my raspberries before they get squishy! One solution is to visit your local farmers' markets and get lovely, fresh items when they come out. How about wintertime, though? Another solution which works wonderfully is to keep a few bags of frozen fruits and berries in re-sealable containers in the freezer. That way any time you'd like a sangria you just reach into the freezer, grab a handful of an appropriate fruit or berry mix, and enjoy.

Herbs

Ginger works wonderfully in sangrias, adding a spicy kick to the flavor. Orange peel is another great item to add into sangria for a zesty taste. Several people swear by mixing in cinnamon red hots for that cinnamony spiciness.

Ice Cubes

Sangria is best served cold! In addition to water-based ice cubes, look into getting the plastic washable ones. That way they keep your drink nice and cold, but don't dilute your sangria flavors.

Sangria Recipes

Sangria Instructions

Sangria is not complicated like a layered drink or a flaming drink. Making a sangria recipe is about relaxing, having fun, and enjoying life!

Chilled Ingredients
Sangria is meant to be served cold, so it works best if the wines and ingredients you use are chilled. The liquor does not need to be chilled, but the wine and fruits should be.

Chop Up the Fruits and Berries
Sangria is easiest to drink when the fruit and berry components are small and easy to drink while you're drinking the liquid part. On the other hand, though, it does look really pretty if you have a large strawberry floating in the glass, for example. So balance your desire for easy eating with your enjoyment of the visual appeal.

Mix Well and Let Soak
If you can at all plan for it, try to let your sangria mixture sit overnight in a fridge. That way all the delicious flavors from the fruits and berries can soak into the sangria and permeate it. This means the sangria you drink the next morning will have all the natural fruit juices integrated into it.

Add any Bubbly / Sparkly Items Last
If you are adding in club soda, sparkling wine, ginger ale or anything else with bubbles, put that in at the very last moment. Don't put that in before an overnight soak. Otherwise all your bubbles will be lost and will go flat before you get a chance to enjoy it.

Sangria Recipes

Have Fun!

Sangria is about enjoying your friends, family, and the natural world around you. Mix things up. Use a white wine instead of a red. Use cherries instead of blueberries. Do whatever strikes you as interesting, and explore the results!

Sangria Recipes

Sangria Glassware

What do you drink your sangria out of? Sangria is all about fun and relaxing, to the answer is as varied as the people around the world. You can drink sangria out of a tall thick glass, out of a wine glass, out of a footed glass, and just about anything else you can dream up.

Here are some suggestions from my years of sangria drinking!

Copas Hand-blown Recycled Glass

I love that this glassware is made in Spain, birthplace of Sangria. I also love that it is made from recycled glass. You get four glasses in this set, each holding 12 ounces of your favorite sangria. This does far better than those tiny 5oz wine glasses! Perfect for adding in wheels of lemon and lime to create a gorgeous presentation.

Spanish Wine Glasses

If you watch movies like The Godfather or other movies involving European culture, you'll find that most people did not use fancy, high end lead-crystal glassware to relax on their back porch and watch the sun set. They used sturdy, hard-working solid glassware that would stand up to daily use. These glasses are exactly the perfect style for sangria. You can hang out with friends, put up your feet, and be yourself.

Sangria Recipes

Sangria Pitchers

Are you a fan of Sangria? Unless you are making giant bowls of sangria for a party, your best bet is to make it up a pitcher at a time. That way you keep it in the fridge - so the fruit stays relatively fresh - and can pour it out by the glass whenever you'd like some.

Traditional sangria pitchers have a pinched pour spout. This is there to catch the fruit bits, so that they don't "plunk out" into your glass and make a big splash. You want to keep the fruit inside the pitcher, flavoring the liquid there, and only pour out the pre-flavored liquids in your glass to enjoy.

Most sangria pitchers are made from a ceramic. That way the ceramic acts as a natural insulator and helps to keep the sangria cool on a hot summer's day. In modern times, when people sometimes drink sangria in the winter as well, the pretty see-through glass variety of pitcher can also be quite lovely.

Throughout this book are images of great pitchers to serve your sangria in. I own the two of the ceramic ones myself and really love it. All of them are hand made in Spain and have a regional flair to them. If you get multiple pitchers you can keep one in the fridge so your sangria is fresh and ready, while the other one is being cleaned out! These are all offered by Tienda.com – a Spanish themed store I highly recommend.

Sangria Recipes

Sangria Toasts

Have some fun with different toasts from around the world! Let me know if you have other toasts to add in to this collection.

Chinese: Ganbei! (dry your cup)

Dutch: Prost! (health)

English: Cheers!

French: Santé! (health)

German: Prost! (cheers)

Hebrew: Le'chaim! (to life)

Irish: Sláinte! (to your health)

Italian: Per cent'anni! (for one hundred years)

Italian 2: Salute (health)

Japanese: Kanpai! (dry your cup)

Russian: Vashe zdorovie! (to health)

Spanish: Salud! (health)

Welsh: Iechyd da! (health)

Americans don't tend to have a single word toast. They normally toast to something in particular - friendship, love, the person at the event, and so on.

Sangria Recipes

There are over a hundred sangria recipes presented here for your reading pleasure. If you're reading the print version of this book, there's a handy index at the back of the book to help you find recipes based on the ingredients you have on hand. If you're using an ebook version, the search function of your system will do the same job just as easily.

If you have a favorite ingredient that I am not using, please let me know! I am always working to improve and enhance my sangria offerings.

Sangria Recipes

Sangria Creation Tips

Most of the recipes in this listing are presented in single serving size. If you want to create a party serving of that sangria, simply multiply the recipe by four. A bottle of wine has about four glasses of wine in it, so multiplying by four should give you the value for one 750ml bottle of wine and the associated ingredients to go with it.

A few of the recipes are listed at party size to start with. Often these are recipes with numerous ingredients or other complicated aspects to them. If you would like to give a single serving a shot, then you'd go the opposite direction – divide by 4 to reduce a bottle down to a glass size.

For just about any fruit mentioned here, you can toss some in the freezer to act as natural ice cubes for your sangria. For example, I keep frozen peaches, raspberries, and strawberries in my freezer. That way when I'm ready for a sangria I can add a few of those to my drink, for both flavor and to keep it cool.

Keep in mind, though, that a frozen fruit item won't absorb the flavor as well. So if you have access to fresh fruit, it's good to make most of the fruit component be fresh.

Also, if you have time, it's well worth it to let your sangria sit and marinate for a while, even if it's just a half hour. That will let the flavors of the fruit meld in with the liquid and vice versa. Just be sure to add any bubbly or sparkling component to the sangria right before serving. That way the bubbles don't get lost.

Sangria Recipes

Absolut Vodka Sangria Recipe

This is a very potent recipe, so make sure there are designated drivers (or lots of floor space for sleeping). The combination of fruit flavors along with the orange juice and Triple Sec (an orange flavored liqueur) bring a mouth-bursting flavor to this sangria recipe.

Ingredients
1 bottle red wine
1 bottle 7-up
1 bottle orange juice
1/2 cup brandy
1/2 cup Triple Sec
1 bottle Absolut Vodka
1/8 cup lime juice
2 apples
2 oranges
2 grapes

Prepare a large pitcher or bowl. Pour in the red wine, orange juice, brandy, Triple Sec, vodka, lime juice. Add in the apples, oranges and grapes. Let the mixture sit in the fridge for at least two hours, and preferably overnight so the fruit flavors all soak into the liquids.

Before serving, add in the 7-up so the bubbles are fresh. Serve over ice. If you have extra fruit, freeze the pieces to act as natural ice cubes.

Apple Artichoke Sangria Recipe

We all know about apples and their health benefits. But did you know the artichoke is actually the base of a purple thistle flower? In the wild it has a bushy purple flower coming out of its top! Very cool. This recipe provides two staple ingredients that used to keep people fed through a long winter.

Ingredients
1/4 apple cut up
1oz artichoke liqueur
1 glass red wine

Chop the apple up into small slices so you can drink them in while you drink the sangria. Or, if you're less picky, you can use your fingers to pluck them out. Pour in 1oz of the artichoke liqueur. The brand I have is Cynar but there are probably other brands out there as well. Fill the wine glass up with red wine, and enjoy!

Sangria Recipes

Apple Orange Sangria Recipe

The image of apples and oranges is a pretty classic one! These flavors go really well together, and the sangria they create is quite out of this world

Ingredients
3oz shiraz (fruity red wine)
1oz Bacardi big apple rum
1oz orange juice
1oz Triple Sec
1oz club soda
Orange wheels

Pour all ingredients into a large glass over ice. Add in a few wheels of orange plus a lime wedge. Mix it all together and enjoy!

Sangria Recipes

Apple Lychee Sangria Recipe

An apple a day keeps the doctor away! Apples are good for you and come in a variety of colors. Lychee liqueur adds a delicious exotic sweetness to the mix. Lychees are sweet fruits that hail from China. They have a delicious sweetness much like a grape!

Ingredients
1/4 apple cut up
1oz lychee liqueur
1 glass white wine

Cut the apple into small slices so you can eat them as you drink. Put them into a wine glass. Add in the lychee liqueur. Finally, top the glass off with a white wine. Chenin blanc is the classic white to use because it has an apply flavor, but any white should do nicely. It's best if the white wine is rather cold - otherwise, toss in some plastic ice cubes to cool things off.

Sangria Recipes

Basic Sangria Recipe

Sangria is the perfect summer drink. Sangria at its core is a mix of red wine, fruit, and hard liquor. Think of it as fruit punch for the adults. This is a great one to prepare the night before, for your summer picnic party.

Ingredients
1 bottle Rioja or other red wine
1 shot glass of lime juice
2 shots Bacardi rum
Random fruit as desired

This is about as easy as it gets for Sangria. Customize your sangria recipe with things you like!

Mix all ingredients together and chill in the fridge overnight if possible, so the fruit flavors soak into the alcohol. The next morning, toss in some ice cubes and serve!

Sangria Recipes

Berry Blend Sangria Recipe

Berries are the ultimate summertime treat. This sangria recipe mixes together some of the best berries to create the ultimate flavor combination!

Ingredients
2 strawberries, sliced
2 blackberries
5 raspberries
5 blueberries
1 glass chardonnay

Refrigerate all items ahead of time so they're nice and cold. Chop up the strawberries into bite-sized pieces if you wish. You can also leave them whole for more of a visual appeal. Put the strawberries, blackberries, raspberries and blueberries into a glass. Fill with chardonnay. This works best with a fruity chardonnay rather than a minerally chardonnay.

You can buy frozen "berry blend" mixes in the grocery store. This makes it easy to just scoop out a few of them each time you want to make sangria. They act as natural ice cubes for your drink!

Sangria Recipes

Blackbeard Berry Sangria Recipe

Blackbeard was a famous pirate who terrorized the oceans in the 1700s. Many felt he was insane. It makes sense that Absinthe - a liquor thought to promote insanity - is featured in his berry sangria recipe. Yar! Live life like pirate, live each day to the fullest, and nibble on a strawberry while you're at it.

Ingredients
1oz Absinthe
1oz blackberry liqueur
strawberries
1 glass red wine

Put the Absinthe and blackberry liqueur into a glass. Add in the strawberries. Fill with red wine.
Toast to the life on the high seas!

Sangria Recipes

Blackberry Blueberry Sangria Recipe

Blackberries and blueberries are both chock full of healthy antioxidants. Add in the Creme de Cassis mixer which is the juice of black currants. This liqueur was created by monks and was thought to cure "wretchedness". :)

You can use any style of red wine you wish, although a spicy variety does better to add to the combination of tastes you get.

Ingredients
5 blackberries
5 blueberries
1 oz Creme de Cassis
1 glass red wine

Refrigerate all items ahead of time so they're nice and cold. Put the blackberries and blueberries into a glass. Add in the ounce of Creme de Cassis liqueur. Fill with red wine.

Blackberry Spice Sangria Recipe

Blackberries, as you'll find I'm fond of repeating, are delicious and full of antioxidants. Just as metal can rust, so can your body be damaged by free radicals. Antioxidants help to combat this problem.

This blackberry spice sangria recipe tantalizes you with a rich plethora of spice flavors in an easy to use container of Captain Morgan's Spiced Rum.

You can use any style of red wine you wish, although a spicy variety does better to add to the combination of tastes you get. Shiraz comes to mind.

Ingredients
5 blackberries
1 oz Captain Morgan Spiced Rum
1 glass red wine

Refrigerate all items ahead of time so they're nice and cold. Put the blackberries into a glass. Add in the ounce of Captain Morgan Spiced Rum. Fill with red wine.

Sangria Recipes

Blueberry Sangria

Blueberries are great in the summertime, and have many health benefits. Tuft's University rated blueberries as #1 in antioxidants when compared with 40 other fruits and veggies in this category. Get your oh-so-important antioxidants in a delightful, refreshing drink!

Ingredients
1 750ml bottle Spanish (or other favorite) red wine
1/3 cup sugar
1 cup apricot brandy
2 cups blueberries
1 cup sliced red grapes
1 cup sliced purple grapes

Prepare a large bowl or pitcher. Mix together the red wine, sugar and brandy until well blended. Add in the blueberries, red grapes and purple grapes. Refrigerate overnight to allow the berry flavors to soak into the mixture.

Serve the next day from a large pitcher filled with ice. Enjoy the delicious antioxidant benefits of the red wine and blueberries! If you have some blueberries left over, freeze them and use them as natural ice cubes.

Sangria Recipes

Blueberry Orange Sangria

Blueberries' antioxidants help you fight cancer, diabetes, heart disease and much more. Even better, blueberries are tasty too!

Orange liqueur adds a nice dash of citrus to this recipe. If you don't have access to Triple Sec, you can substitute in Grand Marnier or Cointreau. Both of these are also orange flavored.

Ingredients
10 blueberries
2 oz Triple Sec
1 glass red wine

Put the blueberries into a wine glass. If you have frozen blueberries they have the added benefit of naturally chilling your sangria! Add in the Triple Sec, then fill the glass with red wine. A merlot works really well here, as blueberry-merlot is a classic flavor combination. Any red wine should do though.

Sangria Recipes

Blueberry Sparkling Sangria

This bubbly, fruity sangria is very easy to make, and is quite delicious. Blueberries are native to North America and in addition to their fantastic antioxidants a serving of blueberries provides 24% of your daily Vitamin C. The Chambord adds in a nice raspberry tartness.

If you keep frozen blueberries in your freezer not only are you always ready to whip some of this up, but the blueberries also act as natural ice cubes floating in your glass.

Ingredients
1 750ml bottle sparkling wine
4 shots Chambord raspberry liqueur
2 cups blueberries

Pour the bottle of sparkling wine into a pitcher. Add in the Chambord and the blueberries. You want to serve this immediately so the bubbles don't diminish. Alternately, you can soak the Chambord and blueberries overnight first - so the flavor of the blueberries gets into the liquid - and then add that to the sparkling wine right before you serve it.

I tend to use Asti Spumanti which is an Italian sparkling wine - this gave it a sweeter flavor. If you like a more dry style, then certainly go for a traditional French Champagne instead.

Sangria Recipes

Bombay Sapphire Sangria Recipe

Bombay Sapphire is a delicious gin in a beautiful bottle. The combination of flavors is great on this sangria recipe! It's unusual because it combines together red wine and white wine in one blend. The mixture works best if both are light, fruity wines.

Ingredients
1 750ml bottle white wine
1 750ml bottle red wine
1 orange, segmented
1 lemon, sliced
2 peaches, sliced
10 grapes
4oz Bombay Sapphire gin

Prepare a large bowl or pitcher. Pour in the white wine, red wine, orange, lemon, peaches, and grapes. Mix in the gin.

Refrigerate and allow to soak for at least two hours, preferably overnight. This allows the flavors of the fruits to permeate the sangria.

Serve over ice. If you have some spare fruit bits, freeze them to use as natural ice cubes.

Sangria Recipes

Brenda's Sangria Recipe

This recipe was kindly donated to our project by Brenda, one of our fans! The notes are her own.

My favorite fast and easy Sangria recipe for parties is to use a big jug of Sangria from the market, by, I don't know... E & J Gallo?

I add 7-up, orange/tangerine juice, and toss in chopped apples and oranges, mixed melon pieces and some of the peel from the apples. And ice, of course.

People drink it more than anything else at my garden parties.

So in a more straightforward way you have:

Ingredients
1 750ml bottle premixed sangria
1 2 liter bottle 7-Up / Sprite
2 cups orange juice
1 apple, chopped
1 orange, segmented
1 cup melon pieces

Prepare a large pitcher or bowl. Pour in the sangria mix, then add in the 7-up, orange juice, apple, orange, and melon. Stir well. Let sit for a few hours if possible so the liquid absorbs the fruit flavors. Serve with ice.

Sangria Recipes

Brown Sugar Sangria Recipe

Every time I hear the name "brown sugar" I think of the popular song by the Rolling Stones. This sangria's delicious flavor will get you up and dancing!

Ingredients
1 750ml bottle red wine
juice of 2 fresh squeezed oranges
juice of 2 fresh squeezed lemons
juice of 2 fresh squeezed limes
1 tsp Brown Sugar
2 cups of Ginger Ale

Prepare a large bowl or pitcher. Add in the red wine, orange juice, lemon juice, lime juice and brown sugar. Allow to soak for several hours or overnight so the liquid absorbs the fruit flavors.

When ready to serve, add in the ginger ale so the bubbles are fresh. Decorate with orange wheels.

Sangria Recipes

Catherine the Great Sangria Recipe

Catherine the Great was an amazing ruler, keeping charge of Russia for an astonishing 34 years. She brought stability and power to Russia, modernized the culture, and promoted education for women. This delightful sangria in her honor features the pomegranate - long a sign of female strength - as well as the traditional Russian vodka!

Ingredients
1oz vodka
1oz pomegranate liqueur
peaches
1 glass red wine

Put the vodka and pomegranate liqueur into a glass. Add in the peaches. Fill with red wine.

Na Zdorovie!

Sangria Recipes

Champagne Sangria Recipe

In Spain for a sparkling sangria recipe they would use cava, which is the Spanish sparkling wine. However, they also like French Champagne in Spain as well, so feel free to use that or any other sparkling wine you enjoy.

Ingredients
3oz Triple Sec
3oz brandy
2oz rum
2oz vodka
1 cup strawberries, blended
chopped up fruit as desired (apple, mango, tangerine, pear, peach)
1 750ml bottle sparkling wine

Prepare a large bowl or pitcher. Add in the Triple Sec, brandy, rum, vodka, strawberries, and fruit. Mix together well. Allow to sit for at least a few hours, and preferably overnight, so the liquids soak up the flavors of the fruits you have chosen.

Add in the sparkling wine just before serving, so that it doesn't go flat.

This sangria has quite a kick, so take that into account!

Sangria Recipes

Cinco de Mayo Sangria

Cinco de Mayo celebrates The Day of the Battle of Puebla – when, on May 5th, the Mexicans won an against-the-odds victory against the French. A lovely time to celebrate the Mexican culture!

Ingredients
4 cups dry red table wine
2/3 cup freshly squeezed orange juice
1/4 cup freshly squeezed lime juice
1/2 cup caster sugar
2 limes or 1 apple, sliced, to serve

Half fill a large jug with ice cubes. Pour in the wine and the orange and lime juices.

Add the sugar and stir well until it has dissolved. Pour into tumblers and float the lime or apple slices on top.

Serve at once.

NOTE: Caster sugar is a very fine sugar, although not as powdery as confectioner's sugar. It's used in drinks because it dissolves easily. If you only have normal sugar, grind it up a bit in your food processor.

Sangria Recipes

Cinnamon Anise Sangria Recipe

Two great tastes that taste great together! The anise flavor comes from the classic Absinthe - banned for many years because it was thought to be "dangerous". The cinnamon comes from the gold flake filled Goldschlager from Germany.

Ingredients
1 shot Absinthe
1 shot Goldschlager
Red wine
frozen raspberries

Pour the shot of Absinthe and shot of Goldschlager into a wine glass. If you want a lighter flavor, you can use just a half shot of each one. Pour in the red wine to fill. Here I'm doing it with a Georgian wine - Khvanchkara - but you can use any type you enjoy. For tradition, you can of course go with a Spanish Rioja.

Add in the frozen raspberries to add a chill without diluting the flavors. Give a little swirl, and enjoy!

Sangria Recipes

Cinnamon Red-Hot Sangria Recipe

This is a party favorite from deep in the heart of Florida. :) Stacey kindly donated her recipe to our project! Thanks, Stacey! If you like cinnamon red hots, you're in for a treat here.

Ingredients
1 750ml bottle Gallo hearty Burgundy (or other similar light, fruity red wine)
1 can Red Hawaiian Punch
1 lemon, cut up
1 orange, cut up
1 small bag cinnamon red hots
1 one-liter bottle club soda

Pour the red wine into a large pitcher or bowl. Add in the Hawaiian Punch. Next add in the lemon, orange, cinnamon red hots and club soda.

Mix all together and refrigerate overnight.

When serving, pour over ice and add fresh fruit for visual appeal.

Sangria Recipes

Cognac Sangria

Cognac is a specialty brandy created in Cognac, France. You can substitute in regular brandy if you don't have any cognac around. The apples, oranges and cherries add a delightful fruitiness to this sangria!

Ingredients
1 750ml bottle of red wine - Rioja, or other substitute
3oz Cognac
1/4 cup sugar
1 apple, in chunks
1 orange, in wedges
10 cherries
1 liter soda water

Prepare a large bowl or pitcher. Pour in the red wine. Add in the Cognac, sugar, apple, orange and cherries. Mix it well, then allow to sit overnight to let the flavors soak in.

The next day, add in the soda water so the bubbles are fresh. Add in ice and serve! If you have some fruit pieces remaining, use them as natural frozen ice cubes!

Sangria Recipes

Cranberry Orange Sangria Recipe

This recipe is perfect for Thanksgiving, the holidays, or for celebrating anything having to do with Massachusetts or New England. Since it uses white zinfandel, it's very light and fruity. Perfect for all types of events!

Ingredients
1 cup water
1/2 cup sugar
3 whole cloves
1 cinnamon stick
3 lemon slices
4 cranberry herbal tea bags
1 750ml bottle white zinfandel wine
2 to 4 tablespoons brandy
1/2 pint strawberries, trimmed
1 orange (unpeeled) in 1-inch chunks
1 cup club soda

In a small saucepan combine the water, sugar, cloves, cinnamon stick, and lemon. Bring to a simmer over medium heat, then reduce heat to low. Simmer another 10 minutes. Remove pan from heat.

Add in the cranberry herbal tea bags, and let sit for 5 minutes. Now remove the solids with a slotted spoon.

Refrigerate the tea mixture until cool. Put into a large serving container. Add in the wine and brandy. Now add orange and strawberries. Cover and refrigerate overnight.

Just before serving, add in the club soda so the bubbles are fresh while drinking. If you have some extra strawberries, freeze them and use them as natural ice cubes!

Sangria Recipes

Cranberry Peach Sangria Recipe

Fresh and fruity, this sangria recipe is perfect for fall get-togethers with family and friends! It's light and fruity, with gentle flavors that all can enjoy.

Ingredients
1 750ml bottle white zinfandel / rose wine
3 cups cranberry juice cocktail
4 peaches, cubed
1 lemon, wheeled

Prepare a large bowl or pitcher. Add in the white zinfandel, cranberry juice, peaches, and lemon. Refrigerate at least an hour to combine the flavors, or ideally overnight.

Serve over ice. If you have some extra peaches, freeze the cubes to act as natural ice cubes.

Cranberry Sangria Mold Recipe

Watch it wiggle - see it jiggle! Molds are great fun to eat, and this one has the delicious flavor of sangria. Not for the kiddies. Make sure this one is served to adults only. You can always make a separate mold for the little ones that is alcohol free. Just make sure to mark them very clearly.

Ingredients
2 envelopes unflavored gelatin
1/3 cup sugar
2 cups cranberry cocktail
1 cup red wine
1 peach, cubed
1 orange, cubed
1 tsp lemon peel

In a saucepan, combine the gelatin, sugar and cranberry cocktail. Heat for about three minutes. Add in the red wine, then remove from heat and refrigerate.

Wait for mixture to semi-thicken before adding in fruits, so they don't all sink to the bottom. :)

Pour the Jell-O mixture into a mold and refrigerate until firm.

Sangria Recipes

Cranberry Tangerine Sangria Recipe

Cranberries are full of health benefits and antioxidants. Here's a great way to have a fun sangria recipe drink that's healthy too. Add in some tangerine for a flavorful kick!

Ingredients
10 dried cranberries
1oz tangerine liqueur
1 glass chardonnay

Add the cranberries and tangerine liqueur into a wine glass. Add in chardonnay to fill the glass. The cranberries will plump up like magic, and you have a delicious drink!

If you can't find a tangerine liqueur, then an orange flavored one will do as a substitute - Grand Marnier, Triple Sec or Cointreau work well.

Cranberry Tequila Sangria Recipe

Think of this sangria recipe as a blend of the old and new aspects of Spanish culture. The Sangria is from Spain - and the Tequila comes from Mexico! You can use a white Spanish wine for an added flavor of authenticity.

Ingredients
1 bottle white wine
1 can frozen cranberry concentrate
1 cup tequila
1/2 cup lime juice
1/4 cup sugar
1 lime, wheeled

Prepare a large pitcher or bowl. Add in the white wine, cranberry concentrate, tequila, lime juice, sugar, and lime. Refrigerate at least one hour, ideally overnight, to let the flavors soak into the Sangria.
Serve over ice.

Sangria Recipes

Cranberry Triple Sec Sangria Recipe

This delicious cranberry sangria recipe has the added flavor and kick of Triple Sec - an orange flavored liqueur. If you want to make this even more yummy, substitute Grand Marnier for the Triple Sec!

Ingredients
1 750ml bottle chardonnay
1 can frozen cranberry concentrate
1/4 cup Triple Sec
1 orange, cubed
1 lime, wheeled
1 lemon, wheeled
2 cups soda water

Prepare a large pitcher or bowl. Mix together the chardonnay, frozen cranberry concentrate, Triple Sec, orange, lime, and lemon. Refrigerate at least an hour. Overnight is better to allow the flavors to soak into the liquid.

Add soda water and ice just before serving.

Sangria Recipes

Cucumber Orange Sangria Recipe

This sangria is like a relaxing spa visit with fresh, relaxing, aromas around you which somehow invigorate you at the same time. Cucumber liqueur might be hard to find - but it's well worth it!

Ingredients
1 shot cucumber liqueur
1 shot Triple Sec
Red wine
frozen raspberries

Pour the shot of cucumber liqueur and shot of Triple Sec into a wine glass. If you want a lighter flavor, you can use just a half shot of each one. Pour in the red wine to fill. Here I'm doing it with a Georgian wine - Khvanchkara - but you can use any type you enjoy. For tradition, you can of course go with a Spanish Rioja.

Add in the frozen raspberries to add a chill without diluting the flavors. Give a little swirl, and enjoy!

If you don't have Triple Sec, other orange flavored liqueurs include Grand Marnier and Cointreau.

Sangria Recipes

Easter Berry Sangria Recipe

Easter is a time of renewal and refreshment, of celebrating with friends and family the beauties of life and the renewal of our love for each other. Here is a delicious Easter berry sangria recipe to help you with your festivities!

Ingredients
1 cup blueberries
2 cups raspberries
1 cup strawberries, cut into pieces
1/2 cup Chambord (raspberry liqueur)
1 bottle sparkling wine / Champagne

Mix together the blueberries, raspberries, strawberries and Chambord. Refrigerate at least an hour. Overnight is better if you're able to spare the time.

When you're ready to serve the sangria, add in the sparkling wine. You want to do this right before drinking so the bubbles stay fresh!

Happy Easter!

Sangria Recipes

Easy Sangria Recipe

At its core, sangria is a Spanish wine punch that only requires three ingredients - wine, fruit, and a bit of liqueur for a kick. So if you're in a casual mood and don't care what you drink as long as it's easy and fun, here is the recipe for you!

Ingredients
1 750ml bottle of wine
1 cup fruit
1/4 cup hard alcohol

Start with the bottle of wine. Whatever you have around will do quite nicely. It can be red, white, pink, sparkling - you name it. Sangria is made from all styles of wine. Go with what is on hand. Pour it into a pitcher or bowl.

Find a random fruit around. Maybe you have a can of pineapples on the shelf. Drain out the syrup and add them in. Do you have a bag of frozen blueberries in the freezer? Give those a try. A good tip for future shopping is to get some cans and frozen bags of fruit and stock your shelves and freezer with them. Fresh fruit is of course wonderful but it can go bad quickly. By having a few standby ingredients in your home, you're always ready when the mood for sangria strikes you.

Next, grab a random bottle of hard alcohol off your liquor cabinet shelf. It can be rum, vodka, brandy, gin, whatever you have around. Flavored items add interest of course - Grand Marnier will bring an orangey goodness to your concoction while a banana liqueur will add some exotic flavors. Whatever you have is fine.

Mix together and enjoy!

Sangria Recipes

Five Fruit Sangria Recipe

If you enjoy a medley of fruit flavors, then this sangria is just for you! It's like having an entire roll of LifeSavers in your mouth. :) You can use any red wine you wish, but with all the fruit flavors in here a fruity wine works best, like a Chianti or Shiraz.

Ingredients
1 750ml bottle red wine
1/2 cup brandy
1/2 cup Triple Sec
1/2 cup sugar
1 orange, wedged
1 lemon, wedged
1 lime, wedged
1 red apple, wedged
1 peach, wedged
1 6 oz bottle club soda

Prepare a large pitcher or bowl. Pour in the red wine, brandy, Triple Sec, and sugar. Add in the wedges of orange, lemon, lime, red apple, and peach. Stir well.

Allow the mixture to sit and soak for 2 hours or more. Overnight works best. When you're ready to serve, add in the club soda and add in fresh ice.

Sangria Recipes

Frozen Orange Apple Sangria Recipe

This recipe is great because you can keep your freezer stocked with the concentrates and always be ready for delicious sangria! Adding the frozen concentrates right before you serve this sangria gives it a wonderful, thick texture.

Ingredients
2 750ml bottles Rioja (or other red wine)
1/4 cup brandy
2 oranges, sliced
1/4 cup cherries
1/4 cup red grapes
1 2-liter bottle ginger ale
6oz can frozen OJ concentrate
6oz can frozen apple juice concentrate
shaved ice to thicken

Prepare a large bowl or pitcher. Mix the red wine, brandy, oranges, cherries and red grapes together. Let it sit overnight in the fridge to soak.

The next day, mix in the ginger ale, frozen OJ, and frozen apple juice. Stir well. If desired, add in some extra shaved ice to add thickness to the mixture.

Sangria Recipes

Fruity Sangria Blanca

Sangria with fruit is a perfect summertime drink. What makes it great is that you can customize it to hold your favorite fruits, and get some lovely nutrition as well! Where many sangrias are made with red wine, this sangria recipe is made with white wine to emphasize the fruity flavors.

Ingredients
1 750ml bottle Spanish (or other favorite) white wine
1/3 cup sugar
3/4 cup peach-flavored brandy
6 Tbsp thawed lemonade concentrate
8 oz sliced peaches
1 cup sliced green grapes
1 cup sliced red grapes

Prepare a large bowl or pitcher. Mix together the white wine, sugar, brandy and lemonade until well blended. Add in the peaches, green grapes and red grapes. Refrigerate overnight.

Serve the next day from a large pitcher filled with ice.

Sangria Recipes

Georgia Sangria Recipe

Georgia is a fantastic state which is well known for its peaches. This double peach recipe helps to celebrate the southern hospitality that Georgia is famous for!

Ingredients
1oz peach liqueur
peaches
1 glass white wine

Add the peach liqueur into the glass. Now mix in the peaches. If they are frozen, they will act as natural ice cubes for you. Fill with white wine, and enjoy an evening of gentle comfort!

German Delight Sangria

The Germans are famous for many alcohol related things, including Oktoberfest! This delightful sangria recipe celebrates who other things they are known for - Jagermeister liqueur, and Barenjager honey liqueur.

Ingredients
1 oz Jagermeister
1 oz honey liqueur
raspberries
1 glass red wine

Put the raspberries into a wine glass. If you have frozen raspberries they have the added benefit of naturally chilling your sangria! Add in the Jagermeister and honey liqueur, then fill the glass with red wine. Time for a toast!

Gilligan's Island Sangria Recipe

I grew up watching and enjoying Gilligan's Island. This recipe celebrates Ginger, the movie star, along with the sweetness of Mary-Anne, represented by the peaches! It adds in oranges for tropical flair.

Ingredients:
1oz Triple Sec
1oz ginger liqueur
peaches
red wine

Add the triple sec and ginger liqueur into a glass. Next, add in the peaches. If you keep frozen peaches in the freezer, they can act as natural ice cubes if the weather gets warm. If they're fresh peaches, then you can slice them up into smaller bits to make it easier to suck them in while you drink the sangria. Fill with red wine.

Golden Glow Sangria Recipe

Gold has held great meaning throughout civilization. Some have felt gold's wealth guaranteed stability and security in life. Others felt that the golden glow of sunshine led to great health, which is the ultimate treasure. Let the glow of gold bring whatever it is you seek!

Ingredients
1/2oz Goldschlager
1/2oz ginger liqueur
peaches
red wine

Pour the Goldschlager and ginger liqueur into the glass. Add in peaches. Fill with red wine.

Goya Carbonated Sangria

Normally I am a very strong proponent of making your own sangria. The whole beauty of sangria is that it's made with very fresh fruit, using fruits you adore. Sangria is about local and fresh, just like fresh brewed coffee is about brewing it fresh.

However, that being said, there are times this just isn't feasible. Let's say you're throwing a Mexican themed party for teenagers, and for some reason you have to have the sangria all pre-mixed and not made fresh. This could be a solution for that situation.

I want to say clearly that I have no stake in Goya sales. :) Also, I saw this in the supermarket for at least six months straight and refused to buy it before finally giving in to give it a try. So I am definitely not "pushing" Goya. If anything, I was very hesitant about it and did not believe in the thought of pre-mixed sangria.

So, on to the taste test. The sangria is non-alcohol. That's important to make clear! The definition of sangria is "fruit plus brandy" - so this isn't really a sangria, but a sangria-like soda. It is 100% completely safe for kids. It is a bubbly fruit punch.

That is exactly what it tastes like - a sugary fruit punch.

Its first ingredient is carbonated water. Then the second ingredient is high fructose corn syrup. It has 43g of sugars per serving. It has a dose of "natural flavors" (no indication of what) and then caramel colors, preservatives. And Red Dye #40.

So what is my summary? I'm strongly against ingesting lots of high fructose corn syrup. But I understand the realities of life. If you are feeding teenage kids a "Mexican meal" and can't make fruit punch fresh, this might be your only alternative. And in that case, it is fruity tasting and has a light bubble to it. It tastes fine. But if at all possible, make a fresh fruit punch for them. It's far more authentic, far more healthy for them, and much more in the spirit of what Sangria is all about.

Sangria Recipes

Grand Marnier Sangria

I had this at a local, classy fish restaurant (the Naked Fish). It was really quite tasty so I asked for the recipe. Here's how you create a Grand Marnier Sangria, with lots of fruit and orange flavor!

Grand Marnier is an orange flavored liqueur. You can substitute in Cointreau or Triple Sec.

Ingredients
1 750ml bottle Woodbridge Cabernet
4 shots Grand Marnier
6 cherries, sliced
2 oranges, segmented
1 lemon, quartered
1 lime, quartered

Mix together the red wine, Grand Marnier, cherries, oranges, lemon and lime in a large bowl or pitcher. Allow the sangria to sit for a few hours. Strain and serve over ice.

Sangria Recipes

Grape Sangria

Wine is made from grapes. Grapes are tasty to eat! Grapes are enjoyed all over the world. The Greeks and Romans adored grapes, and in North America the muscadine grape grew wild everywhere.

This grape sangria recipe is quite simple and lets you enjoy the classic combination of grapes and wine.

Ingredients
8 grapes
1 glass white wine

This is about as easy as it gets for Sangria. Chop the grapes in half so that they're easier to drink in while you drink your wine. Add in cold white wine - Chardonnay works well - to fill the glass. If you want to add in a liqueur or hard alcohol (vodka, rum etc) then feel free to do so.

Note that unlike other fruits and berries, grapes will promptly sink to the bottom of the glass and start soaking up all the wine. This means to "eat" them you have to wait until you finish your wine and then shake them out of the bottom of the glass. Alternatively, you can have a toothpick spear available and grab them out with that as your wine level gets lower.

Sangria Recipes

Halloween Party Sangria

Halloween, celebrated on October 31st of each year, is the time to explore your dark side! This is a blend of All Saint's Day and Samhain. Both celebrate respecting your ancestors and thinking about those who have passed on.

Use your imagination to make this Halloween punch exceptionally creepy.

Ingredients
2 750ml bottles Rioja or merlot red wine
15oz Cranberry juice
4oz rum
1 cup peeled green grapes

Mix together the red wine, juice and rum until well mixed. Add in the peeled grapes, and refrigerate overnight.

Serve the next day from a large punch bowl. Tell your guests that the peeled grapes are eyeballs, to go with the Halloween theme. The red liquid can be something equally icky, like blood!

Decorate with red and black streamers and other Halloween themed paraphernalia.

Sangria Recipes

Halloween Kid-Friendly Party Sangria

Since Halloween is a kid friendly holiday, I decided to develop a non-alcoholic version of a Halloween sangria for the kiddies.

Please just make sure, if you have both an alcoholic and non-alcoholic version of sangria available at your Halloween festivities, that you put the two drinks far apart. Make it clear which is for adults only! You wouldn't want to have any confusion here.

Ingredients
2 2-liter bottles red ginger ale
15oz cranberry juice
1 cup peeled green grapes

While Sangria is traditionally about wine and brandy, here's a non-alcoholic version for the kiddies. Mix the ginger ale and cranberry juice. Add in the peeled grapes, and refrigerate overnight.

Serve the next day from a large punch bowl. Tell the kids that the peeled grapes are eyeballs, to go with the Halloween theme! The red liquid can be something equally icky, say blood, or maybe just "bug juice" if the kids are little.

For even more fun, toss in some glowing ice cubes! I love these things, I have them in all colors. Every time I have a party with the glowing ice cubes, a few leave with my guests.

Hot Sangria Recipe

Do you like it hot, hot, hot? Are you planning a BBQ where things get spicy? This sangria will be the perfect partner to your dishes!

Triple Sec is an orange flavored liqueur. You can substitute in Cointreau or Grand Marnier which are also orange liqueurs.

Ingredients
1 750ml bottle red wine, preferably Rioja
1 Tbsp lime juice
1 lemon, in wedges
1 Tbsp orange juice
1 orange, in wedges
1 Tbsp sugar
1 shot brandy
1 shot Triple Sec
1 tsp hot sauce
1 bottle sparkling water

Prepare a large bowl or pitcher. Mix together the red wine, lime juice, lemon, orange juice, orange, sugar, brandy, Triple Sec and Hot Sauce. Let chill overnight.

In the morning, mix in the sparkling water. Be sure to do this last so it does not go fast overnight. Add in some ice. It works well to use frozen lime and orange juice cubes to prevent dilution.

Imperial Peach Sangria Recipe

In the Chinese Imperial court, lychees were treasured. These delectable little fruits were considered a special delight. Add in the peach, always treasured in China. Float it in a lovely rose drink, and you've got a delight!

Ingredients
1oz lychee liqueur
peach
1 glass rose wine

Pour the lychee liqueur into a glass. Add in peach and then fill with rose wine. Wrap yourself in silk and watch the clouds drift across the sky!

Sangria Recipes

Italian Restaurant Sangria

I've loved the sangria made by an Italian restaurant (ahem, an Olive Garden) near us. Finally we went there one night with friends and had a few each, to get the flavor. We then experimented until we came up with a rather good approximation. If you love Italian food, give this one a try! It's very fresh, light and fruity!

Grenadine is a non-alcoholic pomegranate-based red mixer.

Ingredients
2 750ml bottles fruity red wine (Chianti works well)
15oz cranberry juice
10oz Grenadine
8oz Sweet Vermouth
5 cherries
1 orange, wheeled

In a pitcher or large bowl, add in the red wine, cranberry juice, grenadine and sweet vermouth. Stir well. Add in a few cherries and orange circles.

Let sit overnight in the fridge if possible. Serve over ice the next day, and enjoy!

Sangria Recipes

Irish Whiskey Sangria Recipe

Celebrate the luck of the Irish with this Whiskey-based Sangria! Many Irish I've met enjoyed making plum wine the 'natural way' when they were teenagers. They would gather up plums put them into a ceramic jug and bury that for a few months. Natural yeasts would do their work and when the jug was pulled up, voila! Cheap wine for singing and dancing.

This Sangria celebrates the fun of Ireland.

Ingredients
1 bottle (750ml) red wine - Rioja, or other substitute
1 bottle (2 liter) Sprite
4 cups Irish whiskey
4 plums, cut into small pieces
1 cup sugar
1 can (12oz) lemonade concentrate

Prepare a large pitcher or bowl. Mix together the red wine, Sprite, Irish whiskey, plums, sugar, and lemonade.

Chill overnight if at all possible. This will let the flavors of the plum permeate the sangria.

Sangria Recipes

Jay's Secret Sangria Recipe

Jay is a bartender who kindly donated his recipe to our website. This recipe makes a huge amount of Sangria - Jay did this for a bar somewhere in Massachusetts - so prepare for a big party!

Ingredients
4 750ml bottles cabernet sauvignon, warm
1 750ml bottle white zinfandel, warm
3/4 quart orange juice
2 small cans pineapple juice
1/4 cup Grand Marnier
3 oranges, wheeled
3 limes, quartered
6 strawberries, halved
1 can Sprite

Get a large bucket or container. Pour in the cabernet sauvignon, white zinfandel, orange juice, pineapple juice, Grand Marnier, oranges, limes, and strawberries. Let it sit warm for about 2 hours.

Now it's time for the full soak. Get it into a refrigerator or cooler and let it set overnight.

In the morning, add in the Sprite. That way the fizziness of the Sprite stays fresh. When serving, pour over ice and add fresh fruit.

To turn this into a smaller portion sangria recipe, a typical assumption is that one 750ml bottle of wine yields four large glasses of wine. Divide all ingredients shown by four. If you're making just a small amount's worth you probably don't want to wait for the overnight soaking.

Sangria Recipes

June Musings Sangria Recipe

The merry month of June brings us gentle breezes, warm sunshine, and delightful weather for relaxing. Add in some cucumber liqueur, a hint of red raspberries, and you have an afternoon to savor.

Ingredients
1oz cucumber liqueur
raspberries
red wine

Add the cucumber liqueur into a glass. Add in the raspberries. If you keep frozen raspberries in the freezer, they can act as natural ice cubes if the weather gets warm. If you have access to fresh raspberries, those can be quite tasty. Now fill the glass with red wine.

Key Lime Sangria Recipe

Key limes are tiny little times that are found on Key West, Florida. The tiny key deer are very cute down there too. This key lime sangria is wonderful with chardonnay - it's even better if you can get your hands on some Key Lime Wine!

Ingredients
3 key limes
1 glass chardonnay (or key lime wine)

Key limes are very tiny, so they can be hard to cut into wheels. I'll usually make an attempt to wheel one of them just for the edge-of-glass display. The rest I'll just cut in half and plunk into the glass. Fill the glass with chardonnay. This works best with a fruity chardonnay rather than a minerally chardonnay.

If you have access to Florida wineries - either in person or via the internet - track down some Key Lime wine! It's very tasty and it works perfectly as a sangria base.

Sangria Recipes

Kiwi Sangria

Kiwi is a delicious small fruit from China about the size of an egg. The outside is a fuzzy brown, while the inside is a tender green. Interestingly the fruit was named after the flightless bird from New Zealand! It was originally called a "gooseberry" but the sellers figured that the cute name of "kiwi" would do better in many markets. :)

If you do not have pinot noir, any gentle red wine will do.

Ingredients
3 750ml bottles pinot noir
1 2 liter bottle ginger ale
5 kiwis
2 Tbsp lime juice

Peel the kiwis and slice them into wheels. Mix together the red wine, kiwis, ginger ale and lemon juice until well mixed. Refrigerate overnight.

Serve the next day from a large pitcher filled with ice.

Sangria Recipes

Kumquat Berry Sangria Recipe

Kumquats are cute little citrus fruits that are sort of like mini oranges. Unlike oranges, you eat the rind on a kumquat, since it's so thin. The rind is sweet, the inside is sour, and it's a delicious combination! The blueberries add antioxidants and a rich undertone. The Strawberries add in a delicious, fresh flavor.

You can use any style of red wine you wish, although a spicy variety does better to add to the combination of tastes you get.

Ingredients
5 kumquats, sliced in half
5 blueberries
3 strawberries
1 oz tangerine liqueur
1 glass red wine

Refrigerate all items ahead of time so they're nice and cold. Put the kumquats, blueberries and strawberries into a glass. Add in the ounce of tangerine liqueur. Fill with red wine.

Sangria Recipes

Kumquat Blueberry Sangria Recipe

Kumquats are native to China and nearby countries – the fruit's thin rind adds a delightful zing to the drink! Add in some vitamin-C-rich blueberries and you've got a tasty, healthy drink.

You can use any style of red wine you wish, although a spicy variety does better to add to the combination of tastes you get.

Ingredients
5 kumquats, sliced in half
5 blueberries
1 oz tangerine liqueur
1 glass red wine

Refrigerate all items ahead of time so they're nice and cold. Put the kumquats and blueberries into a glass. Add in the ounce of tangerine liqueur. Fill with red wine.

Sangria Recipes

Lemon Sangria

Summertime conjures up images of lemonade stands and fresh lemonade served by the pool. Here's an adult version of lemonade which is very tasty!

Rioja is the traditional red wine to use in a sangria, but any red wine you have around will do fine to substitute here.

Ingredients
1 750ml bottle red wine
4oz Cognac
6oz lemon juice
2 lemons, sliced up
1/2 cup sugar
1 2 liter bottle 7-up

Mix together the red wine, cognac, lemon juice, lemons and sugar in a large pitcher or bowl. Chill overnight.

The next day, add in the 7-up so the bubbles are fresh. Pour the sangria into a large pitcher over ice cubes. Garnish with lemon wheels.

A friend of mine, Nancy, adores this recipe. She mixes it up often to feature at her summer parties. Everyone who attends loves the sangria! It's got a great, refreshing flavor.

Sangria Recipes

Lychee Peach Grape Sangria Recipe

Lychees are sweet fruits that hail from China. They have a delicious sweetness much like a grape! Peaches also originally came from China and are now found all over the world. Grapes are a world-wide phenomenon, being enjoyed by just about every ancient culture that existed.

Ingredients
1 slice peach
6 grapes
1oz lychee liqueur
1 glass white wine

Cut the peach slice into small pieces so that each piece is easily sippable. Cut each grape into halves. Put both into a wine glass. Add in the lychee liqueur. Fill the glass with a cold white wine. Chardonnay works well, but any white wine will do.

I'm not sure if you can see it in this photo, but the peaches will float to the top while the grapes will sink to the bottom. It means you can nibble at the peaches as you drink, but you'll have to wait until the wine level drops to easily get to the grapes. By then they will be nice and soaked.

Sangria Recipes

Mambo Taxi Recipe

A Mambo Taxi is a cocktail made by the Mi Cosina Tex-Mex restaurant chain in Dallas, Texas. They keep the secret of this recipe from all who ask.

However, those with sharp eyes have seen that it's made with the following ingredients!

Ingredients
1 750ml bottle basic sangria
1 packet margarita mix
2oz Chambord (raspberry flavored liqueur)

Pour the sangria blend into a pitcher or bowl. If you cannot find a pre-made sangria blend, then any fruity red wine will do, and add in 2oz of fruit punch plus 2oz of standard brandy.

Next add in the margarita mix and Chambord.

Try out combinations of these three ingredients until you hit a ratio that you enjoy!

Sangria Recipes

Mango Cointreau Sangria Recipe

I love Cointreau. Cointreau is an orange liqueur from France. If you don't have any Cointreau around, you can substitute in Grand Marnier or Triple Sec. Both of these are also orange flavored!

Ingredients
1 small mango
1 orange
1 lemon
1 small lime
1 750ml bottle of Rioja or other red wine
1 1-liter pitcher lemonade
1 shot Bacardi rum
1 shot orange Cointreau
sugar to taste

Prepare a large pitcher or bowl. Slice up the mango, orange, lemon and lime into small pieces and put them into the chosen container. Mix in the wine and lemonade. Drop in a shot of Bacardi and a shot of Cointreau.

Taste this. If you want, toss in some sugar. When it tastes right, let it sit in the fridge overnight to soak in all the fruit flavors.

Serve the next day with ice cubes. If you have fruit slices you can freeze, they can serve as natural ice cubes.

Mary Magdalene Sangria Recipe

Mary Magdalene was one of Jesus' most loyal followers. When other apostles fled, Mary was the one who remained by his side at the cross. She is the first person to see Jesus when he returned. Some records indicate that later in life Mary traveled to France to escape persecution. This recipe begins with the pomegranate, a Biblical fruit representing female strength. It adds in Chartreuse, a French blend of herbs created by religious devouts. Add in the apple!

Ingredients
1oz pomegranate liqueur
1oz Chartreuse
apple
1 glass white wine

Put the Chartreuse and pomegranate liqueur into a glass. Slice the apple up into easy to eat pieces. Fill with white wine.

Toast to loyalty!

Sangria Recipes

Melon Low Sugar Sangria Recipe

Many people are reducing sugar in their diets, for obvious reasons! Sugar adds on the pounds and rots out your teeth. Here's a low sugar version of Sangria that makes a deliciously light punch!

Sparkling Ice is a sugar-free drink mix that comes in a variety of flavors. Look through the selection in your store and choose one that appeals to you.

Ingredients
2 2-liter bottles melon / mango Sparkling Ice
1 750ml bottle rose / white zinfandel wine
1 cup strawberries, sliced

Begin by mixing up two bottles of melon or mango flavored Sparkling Ice. Mix in the rose or white zinfandel. You can balance how sweet or non-sweet the punch is by this wine selection - while most white zinfandels are sweet, most rose are quite dry.

Now add in the strawberries for their luscious flavors and antioxidants, stir, and add ice to chill!

Sangria Recipes

Melon Simple Sangria Recipe

Melon is usually associated with the Caribbean and other tropical locations. They trace back to the days of the Egyptians! Bring a bit of the exotic sweetness into your own world with this delicious sangria! It's quick, easy, and very tasty.

Ingredients
5 pieces melon
1 glass chardonnay

Chill the melon and chardonnay beforehand. Put the melon pieces into the glass. Fill up with chardonnay.

There are many ways you can liven this up if you have other ingredients around. Add in orange peel for flavor. For an added kick, add in an ounce of brandy or Grand Marnier - an orange flavored liqueur from France.

Sangria Recipes

Mexican Sangria Recipe

Kick your sangria up a notch with some delicious tequila and the orange-flavored Cointreau from France. This sangria is perfect with a bowl of nachos and salsa! You can use Rioja from Spain as the red wine if you want to be authentic. Other fruity wines that work well include Chianti and Shiraz.

Ingredients
1 wineglass chilled red wine
1 shot Cointreau
1/2 shot Patron tequila
Juice of 1/2 orange
Juice of 1 lime

Prepare a shaker with ice. Add in the red wine, Cointreau, tequila, orange and lime. Mix thoroughly. Then strain into a glass.
Garnish with an orange wheel. Enjoy!

Sangria Recipes

Mexican Triple Sec Sangria Recipe

Sangria is incredibly popular in Mexico. Here's a sangria recipe supplied by a Mexican bartender I know. Apparently the patrons of his bar are quite addicted to this style of sangria! No wonder; it is quite tasty. The sizes are for a single serving, so it's very easy to mix it up to your exact style and taste requirements.

This sangria is unusual because it mixes in both red and white wine. Usually a sangria is one or the other! Triple Sec is an orange flavored liqueur. Substitutions include Grand Marnier and Cointreau.

Ingredients
2oz pinot grigio (light white wine)
1oz merlot (gentle red wine)
1oz Triple Sec
1oz orange juice
slice orange
slice lemon
slice lime

Pour the white wine, red wine, Triple Sec and orange juice into a large glass over ice cubes.

Add in a slice of orange, a slice of lemon and a slice of lime. Perfect for beating the heat on a hot day!

Sangria Recipes

Midori Sangria Recipe

I love Midori. This fresh, crisp melon-flavored liqueur from Japan brings a delicious sweetness to any drink. It is especially true with a nice sangria!

If you do not have access to a merlot, then any gentle red wine will do.

Ingredients
1 750ml bottle merlot
4 shots Midori
2 oranges, segmented
1 lemon, quartered
1 lime, quartered

Pour the merlot into a large pitcher or bowl. Add in the Midori, oranges, lemon, and lime.

Mix all ingredients together and let sit for a few hours. Strain and serve over ice.

Sangria Recipes

Monk's Retreat Sangria Recipe

Monks were often the last stand to preserve knowledge as darkness fell. They would preserve stories, research, and literature for future generations. Frangelico is a great liqueur from Italian monks and the bottle even looks like a monk with a rope around his waist. Chartreuse is a delightful herbal liqueur created by monks in Italy. Add in some raspberries for delight, and you have a taste to savor on your personal retreat!

Ingredients
1/2oz Frangelico
1oz Chartreuse
raspberries
1 glass white wine

Put the Chartreuse and Frangelico into a glass. Toss in raspberries to add texture. Fill with white wine.
Toast to relaxation.

Sangria Recipes

Mythical Dream Sangria Recipe

Different cultures have different legends and dreams. The Biblical stories celebrate the pomegranate, which was the real fruit in the Garden of Eden. In Japan and China, ginger was thought of as a powerful cure for many of life's ills. In many parts of the world the peach was thought to bring immortality.

Ingredients
1oz ginger liqueur
1oz pomegranate liqueur
peach
1 glass red wine

Pour the lychee liqueur and ginger liqueur into a glass. Add in peach and then fill with red wine. If you have frozen peaches, they can act as natural ice cubes. Feel the infinity of the universe surround you!

Sangria Recipes

Nectarine Sangria Recipe

The Spanish have turned sangria creation into an art form. Here's a typical recipe you'll find in many corners of Spain, mixed up by the pitcherful for long afternoons of relaxation and conversation.

If you do not have access to Rioja, then Chianti or shiraz serve as good substitutes.

Ingredients
1 750ml bottle Rioja (fruity Spanish red wine)
1 750ml bottle brandy
1 2 liter bottle Sprite / 7-Up
1/2 cup nectarines
1/2 cup peaches
1/2 cup melon
1/2 cup oranges
1/2 cup lemons

First, chop up the nectarines, peaches, melon, oranges and lemons and pile those into the bottom of a large pitcher. Note that you can leave out a fruit or two depending on what's available; the idea is to create a "medley".

Fill the pitcher half up with the Rioja. Now add brandy until the pitcher is about 2/3rds full, and top it off with the Sprite.

Stir well with some ice, and enjoy! You can re-top the mix off with more brandy, wine and soda as you drink.

Sangria Recipes

New Spain Sangria

Christopher Columbus sailed from Spain, and when he "discovered" the Americas he began a trend which had a huge impact. It's fascinating to realize that what we think of as "Mexico" is really primarily the Spanish culture. The native Mexicans were assimilated and much of their culture was lost.

So when we think about the world of Sangria, which is a Spanish beverage, it is natural that Sangria would become very popular in this "New Spain" area. Mexico is not known for its winemaking, but it does make several great liqueurs. Tequila is one of those, created in Guadalajara from agave.

Ingredients
1 bottle red wine
1 cup tequila
1/2 cup orange juice
1/2 cup caster sugar
1/4 cup lime juice
2 limes or 1 apple, sliced

Start with a pitcher or large bowl. Add in ice cubes about half way up. Add in the red wine, Tequila, orange juice and lime juice. Mix gently. Now stir in the sugar until it dissolves well.

Pour into thick glasses and toss in a few limes or apples. Serve immediately!

NOTE: Caster sugar is a sugar that dissolves very easily in liquid. For this reason it's often used in drinks. It's more powdery than normal grains of sugar, although not as super-light as confectioner's sugar. If all you have is normal sugar, grind it slightly in your blender.

Sangria Recipes

Orange Simple Sangria Recipe

With just a few basic ingredients in your home you can always create this simple sangria recipe! It's full of Vitamin C, too!

Ingredients
1 750ml bottle Rioja (other red wines will do nicely too)
1/4 cup brandy
1/2 cup Triple Sec
4 slices orange
2 cups orange juice
2 cups ginger ale

Prepare a large bowl or pitcher. Pour in the red wine. Add in the brandy, Triple Sec, orange, and orange juice. Allow to sit in a fridge overnight.

The next day, add in the ginger ale. You want to do this last so the bubbles do not fade. Pour that in over ice cubes and toss in a garnish of fresh fruit. Enjoy!

Sangria Recipes

Parisian Cafe Sangria Recipe

French royalty adored strawberries - the small, red berries that have such a delicious taste. Imagine relaxing on a quiet, sunlit, cobblestone street in Paris, elegant people strolling by, while you sip your sangria. The ginger brings an aura of relaxation, and the red raspberries give it that extra touch of delight!

Ingredients
1oz strawberry liqueur
1oz ginger liqueur
raspberries
1 glass red wine

Pour the strawberry liqueur and ginger liqueur into a glass. Add in raspberries and then fill with red wine. A nice Bordeaux would be perfect!

Sangria Recipes

Patriotic Red-White-Blue Sangria

Independence Day in the United States is celebrated on the Fourth of July. This is when our founding fathers signed our Declaration of Independence to stand apart from Britain. It was an incredibly bold step they took - those men who signed the document were hounded and slain for their action! We should honor and celebrate their sacrifice, and treasure our nation with all its strengths and areas for growth.

The color theme is red, white and blue - you can of course use this same idea for any red-white-blue themed event that you have!

Ingredients
1 750ml bottle fruity white wine
1/3 cup sugar
3/4 cup apricot-flavored brandy
6 tbsp thawed lemonade concentrate
1 cup sliced red grapes
1 cup whole strawberries
1 cup sliced purple (blue colored) grapes
1 cup blueberries

Mix together the white wine, sugar, brandy and lemonade until well mixed.

Add in the red grapes, strawberries, purple grapes and blueberries. Refrigerate overnight.

Serve the next day from a large pitcher filled with ice. The items create a red and blue set of colors floating in a "white" drink! Decorate with flags or streamers. Enjoy!

Peach Sangria

I love peaches. Miss Peach was always a friendly, happy character in the Super Mario games!

This combination of white zinfandel and fresh peach flavor is wonderful to bring a smile to your face and some fun into your world.

Ingredients
1 750ml bottle white zinfandel
1/3 cup sugar
3/4 cup peach-flavored brandy
6 tbsp thawed lemonade concentrate
8 oz sliced peaches

Mix together the blush wine, sugar, brandy and lemonade until well mixed. Add in the peaches, and refrigerate overnight.

Serve the next day from a large pitcher filled with ice. If you have a few spare peaches, freeze the slices to serve as natural ice cubes.

Sangria Recipes

Peachy White Sangria

Summertime is the perfect time for light drinks. Many cultures switch from dark colored drinks in the winter to light colored drinks in the summer. Spain is no exception. While red sangria is often the rule of the day for wintertime drinking, summertime needs something fresher and easier to drink. White wine sangria is perfect!

Peaches are also great for any light summer drink, because they have a fresh, cleansing flavor to them.

For the wine, this traditionally would be made with a Spanish white wine. French styles also tend to go well. The plan is for a dry white, not a buttery Chardonnay.

Ingredients
1 750ml bottle white wine
2 peaches, cut up
1/4 cup Triple Sec

Pour the bottle of white wine into a large pitcher or bowl. Cut up the peaches, removing the pits of course, and add them into the pitcher. Now pour in the Triple Sec. If you don't have Triple Sec, any other orange-flavored liqueur like Grand Marnier will do nicely. Mix them all together thoroughly. Let it sit overnight so the peaches soak up the wine flavors and vice versa.

In the morning, add in more ice and if you have them a few fresh peach pieces. Serve and enjoy your white wine sangria!

Sangria Recipes

Pear Sangria

Pears are a wonderfully rich fruit of summertime. Not too long ago having a pear in the winter was a sign of luxury! If you can find it, there's even a delicious pear liqueur - Poire William - from France which would make this sangria recipe extra decadent. The bottle has an actual pear grown inside it.

If you do not have access to pinot grigio, any crisp white wine will do.

Ingredients
2 750ml bottles pinot grigio
2 pears
2 Tbsp lime juice
1 2 liter bottle ginger ale

Chop the pears into 1" cubes. Mix together the white wine, pears and lime juice until well mixed. Refrigerate overnight.

The next day, add in the ginger ale. You want to add this in last so the bubbles do not all go flat. Serve from a large pitcher or bowl filled with ice. If you have spare pears, you can toss in some frozen pear cubes at this point to serve as natural ice cubes.

Sangria Recipes

Pineapple Sangria

Pineapple is usually associated with Hawaii and warm summer beaches, with palm trees and refreshing breezes. Embark on an exotic vacation with this delicious sangria! If you can't find riesling, any light white wine will do.

Ingredients
1 750ml bottle riesling
1 cup pineapple cubes and juice
1 cup apple juice
2 tablespoons lemon juice
1 2 liter bottle ginger ale

Mix together the white wine, pineapple, apple juice and lemon juice until well mixed. Refrigerate overnight.

Add in the ginger ale the next day just before serving, so the bubbles stay fresh.

Serve from a large pitcher filled with ice. If you can freeze a few of the pineapple cubes, they can serve as natural ice cubes.

Sangria Recipes

Pineapple Simple Sangria Recipe

Think about pineapple. Do you imagine Oahu, lounging on a hammock in a tropical paradise? Pineapples are also the traditional colonial symbol for hospitality. Many homes in Colonial America had a pineapple sign above the door to represent their warm welcome.

Bring a bit of the beauty and friendliness of the tropics into your own world with this delicious sangria! It's quick, easy, and delicious.

Ingredients
5 pieces pineapple
1 glass chardonnay

Chill the pineapple and chardonnay beforehand. Put the pineapples into the glass. Fill up with chardonnay. Enjoy!

There are many ways you can liven this up if you have other ingredients around. Add in orange peel for flavor. For an added kick, add in an ounce of brandy or Grand Marnier - an orange liqueur from France.

Plum Blueberry Sangria Recipe

Plums are delicious fruits hailing from Asia and now grown around the world. Blueberries are deliciously round little treats that are chock full of antioxidants. Combine the two with some blackberry brandy for a dark, wonderful sangria!

I used malbec for this sangria; its dense red flavors meld well with the berry and fruit combo. Feel free to try any of your favorite reds!

Ingredients
10 blueberries
1 plum, sliced up
2oz blackberry liqueur
1 glass red wine

Place the blueberries and plum into a large wine glass. Add in the blackberry liqueur. Fill the glass with red wine. Enjoy!

Many people use ice cubes to chill their sangria - but if you keep some blueberries in the freezer they can act as natural ice cubes without diluting your drink!

Sangria Recipes

Plum Tangerine Sangria Recipe

Plums provide 10% of your daily vitamin C and taste wonderful as well. They are perfect in this red wine sangria recipe. Adding in tangerine liqueur gives the sangria a kick of citrus and extra sweetness. If you cannot find tangerine liqueur, substitute in one of the orange liqueurs - Grand Marnier, Triple Sec or Cointreau.

For the red wine, something soft works best here. I did my recipe with malbec and it was quite tasty! Chianti and Shiraz are other traditional favorites for Sangria.

Ingredients
1/2 plum, cut into small slices
1 oz tangerine liqueur
1 glass red wine

Chill the plum and red wine beforehand. Put the plum pieces into a wine glass. Add in the tangerine liqueur. Fill up with red wine.

Enjoy!

Sangria Recipes

Pluot Python Sangria Recipe

Talk about an intriguing set of flavors in this one! You begin with the pluot, a bizarre cross of plum and apricot with a delicious, tangy flavor. Add into that some elderflower liqueur, which always reminds me of Monty Python and the Holy Grail. Plus some raspberries for good measure. A delightful concoction that is sure to amaze your friends.

Ingredients
1oz elderflower liqueur
pluot
raspberries
1 glass white wine

You'll probably have to plan ahead for this one - most people don't have pluots and elderflower liqueur lying around their house. Put the elderflower liqueur into a glass. Add in a handful of raspberries and some slices of pluot. If you have some frozen raspberries, those become great ice cubes that won't melt to dilute your drink. Fill up with the white wine, and enjoy!

Sangria Recipes

Poire Perfect Sangria Recipe

Poire Williams is the name of a French liqueur which traditionally has a whole pear inside its bottle! They get this feat to happen by putting a bottle over a pear flower bud on a tree and letting the pear literally grow inside the bottle. It's very neat! Add in some peach and ginger, and you have a delightful sangria recipe.

Ingredients
1oz Poire Williams or other pear liqueur
1oz ginger liqueur
peaches
red wine

Pour the pear liqueur and ginger liqueur into the glass. Add in peaches. Fill with red wine.

Poirot Chan Sangria Recipe

This sangria recipe pays homage to two amazing detectives - Hercule Poirot and Charlie Chan! Both characters draw on "unusual" (for the time) ethnicities and helped to expand the realm of detective fiction. Hercule Poirot loved Creme de Cassis - black currant liqueur - while Charlie Chan was fond of ginger dishes!

Ingredients
1 shot Creme de Cassis
1 shot ginger liqueur
Red wine
frozen raspberries

Pour the shot of Creme de Cassis and shot of ginger liqueur into a wine glass. If you want a lighter flavor, you can use just a half shot of each one. Pour in the red wine to fill. Here I'm doing it with a Georgian wine - Khvanchkara - but you can use any type you enjoy. For tradition, you can of course go with a Spanish Rioja!

Add in the frozen raspberries to add a chill without diluting the flavors. Give a little swirl, and enjoy!

Sangria Recipes

Princess Peach Sangria Recipe

I'm a fan of Super Mario from way back. Princess Peach was always a delightful character, smiling, happy. This recipe brings out the best in her! It has double doses of peachy fun, plus some Japanese lychee to enhance the wide-eyed joy.

Ingredients
1oz peach liqueur
1oz lychee liqueur
peaches
1 glass white wine

Add the peach liqueur and lychee liqueur into the glass. Now mix in the peaches. If they are frozen, they will act as natural ice cubes for you. Fill with white wine, and enjoy an evening of fun video gaming!

Sangria Recipes

Raspberry Sangria

I love the flavor of raspberries. This sangria recipe combines the delicious raspberry flavor with red wine and raspberry-flavored liqueur. Chambord is a raspberry flavored liqueur from France. For the red wine, Rioja is most authentic, as it's a delicious red wine from Spain. You can substitute in any other red wine you enjoy. Merlot and shiraz work well here.

For the raspberries, fresh raspberries are always best, especially if you can find locally grown ones. Frozen raspberries have the benefit of being natural ice cubes when a few are added in right before serving.

Ingredients
1 bottle (750 ml) red wine
1 pint raspberries
3 shots Chambord

Mix together the wine, raspberries and Chambord until well mixed. Refrigerate at least an hour, or ideally overnight. This lets the flavors from the raspberries soak into the drink.

Serve the next day from a large pitcher filled with ice.

Sangria Recipes

Raspberry Apple Sangria

Raspberry liqueur is often thought of as being the same as Chambord, but there are other options out there. In this example I use a different raspberry liqueur to create a delicious recipe. I add in fresh, crunchy green apples for a bit of contrast.

Ingredients
1 oz raspberry liqueur
green apple slices
red wine

Pour the raspberry liqueur into a glass. Slice up the apple into pieces depending on your interests. Longer pieces can be picked out with your fingers and nibbled on, while smaller pieces can be drunk as you drink the sangria. Then fill the glass with red wine.

Sangria Recipes

Red Sangria

You might ask, isn't all sangria red? Aha! Here is the fascinating thing about sangria. Sangria is really a generic term in Spanish for a mixture of wine and fruit. It can certainly be a red wine - Spain is famous for its delicious red wines. However, Spain does not make only red wine and red sangria. Spain also makes delicious white wines and sparkling wines. Still, the word "sangria" technically means "bleeding" in the Spanish language, and most peoples' blood is red. :) So a red sangria would be the most authentic one!

If we're going for authentic red sangria, then you want to be using a Spanish red Rioja wine. You want to have oranges as your fruit - Spain is one of the top producers in the world of oranges. On the hard liquor side, Spain is probably best known for its brandy.

Ingredients
1 750ml bottle red Spanish Rioja
1 orange, cut up
1/4 cup Spanish brandy

Pour the Rioja into a large pitcher or bowl. Add in orange pieces. You leave the skins on, so that way if someone wants to take out a piece of wine-soaked orange later and munch on it they have a "handle". Add in the brandy.

Mix all together and refrigerate overnight.

When serving, pour over ice and add fresh fruit for visual appeal. Orange wheels work perfectly for this situation!

This is of course a bare-bones basic recipe for red sangria. Normally you would also add in whatever you found growing in your back yard, be it berries, fruits or whatever. It's a little of this, a little of that.

Sangria Recipes

Religious Fervor Sangria Recipe

This delicious sangria combines the famous "Green Fairy" of Absinthe - which was banned for many years - along with the delightfully monk-made Chartreuse liqueur. The blending of herbal and spicy flavors is delicious!

Ingredients
1 shot Absinthe
1 shot Chartreuse
Red wine
Frozen raspberries

Pour the shot of Absinthe and shot of Chartreuse into a wine glass. If you want a lighter flavor, you can use just a half shot of each one. Pour in the red wine to fill. Here I'm doing it with a Georgian wine - Khvanchkara - but you can use any type you enjoy. For tradition, you can of course go with a Spanish Rioja!

Add in the frozen raspberries to add a chill without diluting the flavors. Give a little swirl, and enjoy!

Sangria Recipes

Roman Empire Sangria Recipe

Elderflower is a delicate liqueur with a long history. It was enjoyed by the Roman Empire citizens! Add in some peaches and grapes - both delights in Rome - and you've got a traditional drink that can have you lounging on a chair. Just convince someone to wave that palm-leaf fan to keep you cool!

Ingredients
1oz elderflower liqueur
peach
grapes
1 glass white wine

Put the elderflower liqueur into a glass. Add in a handful of grapes and some slices of peach. Fill up with the white wine, and enjoy!

Sangria Recipes

St. Patrick's Day Sangria

St. Patrick's Day is a great time to celebrate the wonderful world of the Irish! Irish whiskey is of course a standard treat on the Emerald Isle. Many Irish I know grew up with plum trees around, even making their own plum wine with the simple, bury-fruit-in-a-clay-pot method! Midori is a green liqueur for just the right color!

Ingredients
1 bottle (750ml) sparkling wine - Cava, or other substitute
1 bottle (2 liter) ginger ale
2 cups Irish whiskey
2 cups Midori
4 plums, cut into small pieces
1 cup sugar
1 can (12 oz) lemonade concentrate

Mix all ingredients together, and chill overnight if possible. The overnight soaking helps the plum flavor soak into the drink.
The next day, pour over ice in a pitcher and serve!

Sangria Brandy Recipe

Sangria and brandy are really the perfect combination. Sangria is about creating a wine punch that involves fruit and hard alcohol. Since sangria comes from Spain, the most common hard alcohol there would be Spanish brandy. If you add Spanish brandy into Spanish wine, the result is most definitely a delicious sangria!

Ingredients
1 750ml bottle of red wine
1 cup orange pieces
1 cup grapes, cut up
1/4 cup brandy

Put the bottle of wine into a pitcher. Next add in the oranges and grapes. Spain is the #3 producer of grapes in the world, and definitely one of the top orange producers as well. Both of these are found in high quantities all over Spain. Add in the Spanish brandy, and mix!

Enjoy your extremely authentic Spanish sangria with a selection of tapas!

Sangria Recipes

Sangria with Whatever's Around

This sangria recipe is great if you don't have many ingredients in the house. Sangria can be made with red wine, white wine, and sparkling wine.

Usually you do have lime juice and mint! As long as you keep a little green bottle of lime juice in the fridge along with a container of mint, you're all set!

Ingredients
1 750ml bottle of wine, whatever you have
4 Tbsp lime juice
1 1/2 Tbsp sugar
Random fresh fruit if available
Mint leaf
2oz liqueur if available

Mix all but the mint leaf and let it chill. Pour over ice, add mint leaf, and serve!

You can use any liqueur you've got to give it that kick - rum, vodka, brandy, you name it. It's also a good idea to keep a bag or two of frozen berries or fruit in the freezer. That way you've always got a few to drop into a glass.

Sangrita

Sangrita is a traditional drink of Mexico which features tomatoes, oranges along with spice and lime. It always features Tequila. It seems to me that the name is a play on the combination of the fresh flavors of sangria and the Tequila-based cocktail which is a Margarita. I agree that there isn't any wine in here - but Sangria's name comes from the blood red color of the drink. In Spanish, "sangria" means "bloody". So you definitely have the sangria color here, the Margarita's kick, and a delicious flavor!

This recipe makes a big batch, suitable for storing in the fridge for future use, or sharing with friends at a party!

Ingredients
1 lb tomatoes
1/2 cup orange juice
4 Tbsp lime juice
1 small onion, chopped
1/2 tsp granulated sugar
6 small fresh green chilies, seeded and chopped

salt
Tequila

Prepare a large bowl or pitcher. Peel, seed, and chop the tomatoes. Alternately if you want the easy version, just pour in 16oz of tomato juice. Add in the orange juice, lime juice, onion and sugar. Carefully seed and chop the chilies and add them in. Blend until smooth.

Chill thoroughly or add in ice cubes. You do NOT mix in the Tequila. Rather you pour two glasses per person - one of the tomato blend and one of the Tequila. You drink one, then the other, alternating between the two. You don't glug or shoot them or chase them; it is two separate drinks.

Sangria Recipes

Simple Blueberry Sangria Recipe

The simple sangria recipe is for people who want a quick, easy sangria that does not have to soak overnight or involve 8 different ingredients. This simple sangria recipe only calls for one thing - blueberries - to add to your red wine.

Merlot works best as the red wine here, and berry merlot blends are very common on the wine shop shelves! Any merlot should work nicely. You can of course experiment with other wine brands and styles as well.

Ingredients
1 glass red wine
10 blueberries

The wine is best chilled - even down to fridge temperature. Chop the blueberries at least in half - quarters is even better. It makes them easy to drink with the wine, if they're a small size. It also lets the blueberry juice get into the wine. Stir around a bit to mix in the flavors. Then drink and enjoy!

Boost-Up recommendation:
If you have access to blueberry brandy, add some in for an added kick! Neutral brandy works as well, as it won't affect the flavors.

Sangria Recipes

Sparkling Cranberry Orange Sangria Recipe

Lime, orange and cranberry are flavors that go perfectly together. This makes this recipe about one of the most tasty around! You can use any red wine you enjoy. If you want to go for authentic Spanish flavor, try Rioja, Spain's famous red wine. If you're looking for a generally fruity flavor, Shiraz and Chianti work well.

Ingredients
1 750ml bottle red wine
1 cup orange juice
1 cup cranberry juice
1/2 cup cranberry liqueur
1 lime, wheeled
1 orange, wheeled
2 cups orange sparkling water

Prepare a large pitcher or bowl. Add in the bottle of red wine, orange juice, cranberry juice, cranberry liqueur, lime and orange.
Let refrigerate for at least an hour, or ideally overnight.
Just before serving over ice, add in the sparkling water. That way it retains its fresh bubble!

Sangria Recipes

Spring Sangria Recipe

Springtime is the time for daffodils, crocuses, the fresh buds on leaves and the fresh beauty of sunshine. Sangria is the perfect drink to enjoy this season with! Look for fresh fruits which are part of the bounty of spring! The bubbly Champagne in this recipe helps to brighten your world and wash away the lingering remnants of winter.

If you're going for an authentic Spanish feel, the sparkling wine made in Spain is known as Cava.

Ingredients
3 apricots, cut into chunks
1 cantaloupe, balled
1 nectarine, broken into slices
1/2 cup apricot brandy
1 bottle sparkling wine / Champagne

Find a Tupperware container that can hold about 2 cups of material. Add in the apricot pieces, cantaloupe, nectarine and brandy. Refrigerate at least an hour so the fruit flavors soak into the brandy. Overnight is better.

Add in the sparkling wine just before serving. so the bubbles stay fresh! Happy spring!

Sangria Recipes

Strawberry Sangria

Strawberries and orange is a delicious flavor combination. If you can't get fresh strawberries, frozen ones are quite fine and can double as ice cubes!

Ingredients
1 750ml bottle red wine
1 pint strawberries (fresh or frozen)
1 shots brandy
2 shots blue Curacao

Mix together the red wine, strawberries and blue Curacao (orange flavored liqueur) until well mixed. Refrigerate at least an hour, or ideally overnight.

Serve the next day from a large pitcher filled with ice.

You can use any red wine you want, based on what wines you enjoy. For tradition's sake you can go with Rioja, the famous red wine of Spain. You can also go with a variety of fruity style wines like shiraz or Chianti.

Sangria Recipes

Strawberry Chambord Sangria Recipe

Strawberries are delicious summertime treats. Chambord is a wonderful raspberry flavored liqueur. Together they create a very fresh, tasty sangria!

Ingredients
1 strawberry, sliced
1 oz Chambord
1 glass Chardonnay

Refrigerate all items ahead of time so they're nice and cold. Chop up the strawberry into bite-sized pieces if you wish. Put the strawberry and Chambord into a glass. Fill with Chardonnay. This works best with a fruity Chardonnay rather than a minerally Chardonnay.
Enjoy!

Strawberry Ginger Sangria Recipe

Strawberries are native to North America, and are related to roses! Add in some ginger for an extra kick of flavor.

Ingredients
2 pieces strawberry
1/4 tsp ginger
1 glass chardonnay

Chill the strawberries and chardonnay beforehand. You can leave the strawberries whole for a nice visual impact, or chop them into pieces for more flavor and easier time eating them. Fill up with Chardonnay. Enjoy!

There are many ways you can liven this up if you have other ingredients around. Add in orange peel for more flavor. For an added kick, add in an ounce of brandy or Grand Marnier (an orange flavored liqueur).

Strawberry Lemon Lime Sangria Recipe

Strawberry, lemon and lime must be the perfect trio of summery flavors. Look at all the candies and desserts that feature this combination! Here they combine to create a delicious sangria sensation.

You can make this with either red or white wine depending on your tastes. White wine will be lighter and have the added benefit that you can see the fruit floating around in the glass.

Ingredients
1 750ml bottle red or white wine
1 whole sliced orange
1 whole sliced lemon
1 whole sliced lime
3/4 cup sugar, or more or less to taste
6 oz soda water
3/4 oz Grand Marnier
6-8 fresh strawberries, halved

Slice orange, lemon and lime thinly into pitcher. Pour in the wine, then add the sugar. Stir well. Add in the liqueur and again stir well. Finally add in the strawberries.

Cool overnight in refrigerator. Right before serving add chilled soda water and ice cubes.

Strawberry Melon Sangria Recipe

I adore strawberries, and I adore melons. This combination of flavors is just about perfect for a sangria recipe, to bring fresh summertime flavors into your world!

Ingredients
1 strawberry, sliced
1/4 cup cantaloupe, sliced
1/4 tsp orange peel
1 glass chardonnay

Refrigerate all items ahead of time so they're nice and cold. Chop up the strawberry and cantaloupe melon into bite-sized pieces. Put the strawberry, cantaloupe and orange peel into a glass. Fill with Chardonnay. This works best with a fruity Chardonnay rather than a minerally chardonnay.
Enjoy!

Sangria Recipes

Strawberry Orange Peel Sangria Recipe

Strawberries and orange is a delicious flavor combination. If you can't get fresh strawberries, frozen ones are quite fine and can double as ice cubes!

You have two choices here. One is to use whole strawberries for that cool visual appeal. It's nice to see one or two big strawberries floating in a glass. The other option is to cut the strawberry into smaller bite-sized pieces. That makes it much easier to drink and take in a piece or two with each sip. It also allows the strawberry flavor to better permeate the sangria.

Ingredients
2 strawberries
1/4 tsp orange peel
1 glass chardonnay

Cut or do not cut the strawberries based on your visual and flavorful desires. I use them whole if it's a party where presentation is important, but cut them into pieces otherwise. Add in the orange peel. It almost looks like a snow globe when you first mix it in! Now fill the glass with cold chardonnay. You want to go for a citrusy / fruity chardonnay, not a minerally style. Serve cold!

If you use frozen strawberries you get the added benefit of them chilling your drink, but it also means you have to wait a few minutes for them to that before you can start eating them. :)

Sangria Recipes

Strawberry Raspberry Sangria Recipe

I adore strawberries, and I adore raspberries. This combination of flavors is just about perfect for a sangria recipe, to bring fresh summertime flavors into your world!

Ingredients
1 strawberry, sliced
6 raspberries
1 glass chardonnay

Refrigerate all items ahead of time so they're nice and cold. Chop up the strawberry into bite-sized pieces if you wish. Put the strawberry and raspberries into a glass. Fill with Chardonnay. This works best with a fruity Chardonnay rather than a minerally chardonnay.
Enjoy!

Sangria Recipes

Summer Medley Sangria Recipe

Summertime and the living is easy. Enjoy this delicious medley of flavors including orange, cucumber, raspberry, and cinnamon. The resulting mixture is tasty, and lets you relax in the summertime sun!

Ingredients
1/2oz Goldschlager
1/2oz orange liqueur
1/2oz cucumber liqueur
raspberries
red wine

Pour the Goldschlager, orange liqueur, and cucumber liqueur into the glass. Add in raspberries. Fill with red wine.

Sangria Recipes

Summertime Non-Alcoholic Sangria Punch

Sangria traditionally has wine in it, but this is a non-alcoholic version which is perfect for kids and non-drinkers. It's easy to make and delicious. Enjoy!

Ingredients
1 can Hi-C
1 orange, chopped
1 apple, chopped
1 pear, chopped
4 strawberries, chopped

Choose whatever flavor of Hi-C you enjoy the most. Prepare a large bowl or pitcher and put the Hi-C into that pitcher. Add in the orange, apple, pear and strawberries. Let them soak in the fridge for a few hours, or overnight if you can. This gives the best flavor if the ingredients can all sit for a while.

Serve over ice, and enjoy! If you have some extra fruit, stick them in the freezer and use them as natural ice cubes.

Sangria Recipes

Thanskgiving Sangria Recipe

Thanksgiving is a time of year to celebrate our blessings and to commemorate the values of the past. Applejack was a traditional colonial drink made from apples. Add into that a cherry liqueur and you're all set! There are peaches, too, for sweetness.

Ingredients
1 shot applejack
1 shot cherry liqueur
peaches
1 glass white wine

Add the applejack and cherry liqueur into a glass. Now mix in peach slices. If you chop them up into bite sized pieces, then you can slide them into your mouth as you drink. Fill with white wine. Enjoy!

If you keep frozen peaches in your freezer, while you can't cut them into smaller pieces easily, they can serve as natural ice cubes, which is always a treat in warmer months.

Thistle Sangria Recipe

The thistle is a gorgeous flower - did you know an artichoke is a member of the thistle family? Amazing but true! A purple flower grows out of the top of the artichoke plant. Celebrate beauty with this artichoke liqueur recipe.

Ingredients
1oz artichoke liqueur
green apple
1 glass red wine

Add the artichoke liqueur into the glass. Now mix in slices of green apple. If you use smaller slices, you can drink them down as you drink the sangria. Fill with red wine, and enjoy an ode to beauty!

Tropical Sangria

Bananas are delightfully tropical fruits that are high in potassium. Mix in some peaches and an orange liqueur and you have a sangria that will keep you dancing in a conga line for hours on end!

Ingredients
1 oz banana liqueur
1 oz orange liqueur
peaches
1 glass white wine

Put the peaches into a wine glass. If you have frozen peaches they have the added benefit of naturally chilling your sangria! Add in the orange liqueur and banana liqueur, then fill the glass with white wine. Put on your dancing shoes!

Sangria Recipes

White Sangria

White wine sangria is very popular in Spain, especially on hot days. Where red wine can be a bit heavy, white wine is crisp, clear and refreshing. White wine also gives the visual beauty of the fruit within - you can see them floating around in your drink.

This white sangria recipe involves a bit of cooking - so be sure to plan ahead.

For the wine, this authentically should have a Spanish white. French styles also tend to go well - your aim here is for a dry white, not a buttery chardonnay.

Ingredients
1 cup water
1/2 cup sugar
6 short cinnamon sticks
1 750ml bottle white wine
1 cup sparkling water
1 cup apple juice
1/2 cup orange juice
2 oranges, in wedges
10 cherries
2 apples, in chunks

Heat the water, sugar, and cinnamon sticks until they're simmering. Allow to simmer for 5 minutes, then turn off the heat. Cool back down to room temperature.

Pull out the sticks, and mix in all remaining ingredients. Chill overnight. Pour over ice the next day, and enjoy!

Sangria Recipes

1800s Claret Cup Recipe

Claret is the original name of Bordeaux, the red wine blend from France. This Claret Cup punch recipe was very popular in the 1800s, and was often served at parties. It is in essence an early sangria!

Ingredients
1 bottle Bordeaux
1 lemon cut very thin
4 Tbsp powdered sugar
1/4 tsp grated nutmeg
2oz brandy
3oz sherry wine
1 1-liter bottle of soda water

Prepare a large bowl or pitcher. Add in the Bordeaux, lemon, sugar, nutmeg, brandy, and sherry. Right before serving add in soda water and ice.

It's very neat for me to think about Jane Austen and her family sitting around and enjoying Claret Cup. Certainly in the party scenes Jane writes about in Pride & Prejudice, this is exactly what her heroes and heroines would have been drinking.

This recipe was sourced from *The Home Cook Book*, 1877

1918 Mint Julep Recipe

This mint julep recipe is from the Fannie Farmer cookbook of 1918. It is in essence a red wine sangria.

Fannie Farmer was a Massachusetts woman born in 1857 who developed a flair for cooking. She was a stellar student at the Boston Cooking School. Her amazing books of cooking were wildly popular and changed the way many people cooked and measured.

This red wine sangria recipe is made with Bordeaux wine. Bordeaux is a French blend comprised of mostly Cabernet Sauvignon, Merlot and Cabernet Franc. The British took to calling this blend a "Claret". If you cannot get Bordeaux substituting in a Cabernet Sauvignon should do nicely.

Ingredients
1 quart water
2 cups sugar
12 sprigs fresh mint
1 cup orange juice
1 cup strawberry juice
Juice 8 lemons
1 pint claret wine (Bordeaux)
1 1/2 cups boiling water

Make syrup by boiling a quart of water and sugar twenty minutes. Separate mint in pieces, add to the boiling water, cover, and let stand in warm place five minutes.

Strain out the mint, and add to syrup. Add in orange, strawberry and lemon juices, then cool.

Pour into punch-bowl, add claret, and chill with a large piece of ice; dilute with fresh boiling water.

Garnish with fresh mint leaves and whole strawberries.

Sangria Styles

Sangria comes in a wide variety of styles, shapes, and sizes. Sangria is not just "red wine with brandy and random unknown fruit." Sangria can be a bright sparkling wine full of peaches with delicious spiced rum. Sangria can be a luscious lemony white wine with wheels of lemon and gin. Sangria can be a massive bowl with a ladle in it, wheels of oranges spinning lazily in the candlelit air. Sangria can be a pile of fresh strawberries picked from the back garden, a pair of friends with their feet up, and a jug of homemade wine.

What sangria is simply depends on your mood, the available ingredients and your quest for the time being. You can make an incredibly elegant sangria to match your wedding's theme colors. You can toss together a quick sangria when your best friend comes over to hang out for the afternoon. No matter what your atmosphere or taste buds, there is a sangria just right for that situation!

Here are a number of sangria styles to get your little gray cells exploring the possibilities.

Sangria Recipes

Historic Favorite Sangria Recipes

Sangria as a concept has been around since the days of fruit and wine. Back in the old days, buyers did not buy a "bottle of wine" at a local wine shop. The reason is that wine bottles were not made in standard shapes back then. The technology did not exist. If you bought a hand-made bottle, how could you know for sure it really did hold 750ml of liquid in it? So, just like in modern times when you buy meat, you would go to a winery or other shop. You would bring your *own* container and they would measure out the amount you wanted from a large barrel. That way you could see right in front of you how much was being measured.

The wealthy didn't bother with the middle man. They simply bought entire barrels to "lay down" in their cellars, and servants would draw out enough wine for the day into a lovely crystal decanter. It was nice to be rich!

The poor had a different technique. They simply made their own wine! Many of my relatives have created quite delicious wines out of peaches, plums, and whatever else was handy. The instructions for making your own wine are really very simple and this practice was exceedingly common in most villages. Since the poor already had fruit growing in the bushes, and wine fermenting in their back room, they were all set to combine the two together for some sangria!

So the key is to remember that sangria is a drink that has been enjoyed for centuries. It is not something elaborate that must have item one and item two to work properly. Sangria is about fun, friends, delicious fruit, tasty wine, and enjoying life.

Sangria Recipes

Fruity Sangria Recipes

Sangria and fruit is just about the perfect pairing in the wine world. The deliciously juicy flavors of apple, orange, peach, pear, pineapple and other fruits go wonderfully well with the light, fruity wines in our modern world. In fact, if you're lucky enough to live near a fruit winery, you'll discover that wines made *out* of fruit can be quite delicious!

Ice wines - some of the most expensive wines on the market - often boast flavors of peach, pear and tropical fruits. This is a much highly desired flavor combination in those wines. With sangria you are creating your own ice wine medleys, for far less money!

Fruity sangrias are perfect for summertime sipping, to keep you cool and refreshed. They're also perfect any time you want a tropical break from your daily life. Get some fresh fruit, mix in a delicious wine, and enjoy!

Sangria Recipes

Berry Sangria Recipes

You might think that wine and berries are two different things. Really, grapes *are* berries - so all grape wines are berry wines! Some of my favorite dessert wines are made from blackberries and blueberries. These berries create delicious, rich wines which are tasty and full of antioxidants. Just perfect with a dense chocolate cake.

Adding berries into your sangria can work well in a number of ways. Strawberries with Champagne is a classic combination which has graced many an elegant brunch. Simply add in some brandy (including flavored brandies!) to kick this up a notch. For those who like darker wines, you can combine red wine with blackberries and blueberries for delicious results.

Don't forget the raspberries! With raspberries and Chambord you get the best of all possible worlds.

Sangria Recipes

Spicy Sangria Recipes

Normally sangria is about relaxing with gentle fruity flavors. You start with a light, fruity wine, you add in some tasty fruit, mix in a bunch of ice cubes, and sip quietly in the shade. However, sometimes you want to kick things up a notch and get things spicy.

Some of my favorite sangria recipes fall into this spicy arena. I adore cinnamon red hots, so any recipe that involves those is sure to be a winner in my book! Hot sauce is another surprise ingredient which can really add a kick to your sangria.

Be warned - these recipes aren't for the tame at heart. If you like things quiet and sedate, we've got a lot of recipes for you over in the fruity area. If you're ready for a challenge, though, read on to the spicy recipes!

Sangria Recipes

Luxury Sangria Recipes

Sangria began as a casual, relaxed way to enjoy wine and fruit. It is something that anybody can enjoy who has access to even blueberries and raspberries. Like with all food items, though, sangria can also be enjoyed as a very delicious, high end ingredient luxury.

The key here is both to enjoy the ingredients and the liqueurs. If you get fresh, local apples they can taste *far* more delicious than apples trucked in from across the globe. Long distance fruits are bred to "survive the transportation experience" - usually at the expense of flavor. Many farmers I know talk about how differently a raspberry or peach or strawberry can taste based on when you get it.

So visit your local farmers' markets. Shop locally. Eat foods which were bred for flavor, not for lasting 3 months in a box. Add in some superb liqueurs - Grand Marnier, Cointreau, Chartreuse - and you've got yourself the makings of a drink to remember!

Sangria Recipes

Sparkling Wine Sangria Recipes

I have researched and created over 100 Champagne cocktail recipes. I definitely adore Champagne and I love mixing champagne in with a variety of liqueurs to see what happens. With Champagne Sangria you get an even better challenge - add in fruits! Now you get the bubbly freshness of a sparkling wine, the rich flavors of a delicious liqueur or alcohol, along with the juicy goodness of ripe fruit. I'm not sure anything could be better than this.

The key when you make a Champagne sangria is to think about the timing. Usually with a sangria you want all the fruits and ingredients to soak overnight, so that the flavors of the fruits get out into the liquid area. However, with a bubbly wine, if you let it sit out overnight the bubbles would all go away! So this is a two part process. First, let everything *except* the bubbly wine sit together to join juices. Then, right before you're ready to serve the sangria, pop open the sparkling wine bottle and add that in. That way the bubbles are fresh and active.

One note here. When you open a Champagne or other sparkling wine bottle, the cork should always *ease* out of the bottle. It should come out slowly and gently with a "sigh". You don't want to lose or waste the bubbles!

Holiday Sangria Recipes

A main part of the fun of a holiday is the traditions that you create for it. At Christmas, you always have mistletoe hanging over your doorway into your kitchen. You always have a witch's cauldron by the front door for Halloween to great the trick-or-treaters with. Favorite foods fall into this category as well. You can easily have people waiting months to get their hands on your special Christmas sangria.

The key here is to be imaginative. Is there a color theme for your holiday? Match that theme with your sangria punch! Is there a flavor theme, like strawberries for Valentine's Day? You can easily find a matching sangria to keep that theme going.

With a little creativity you can come up with a sangria for every holiday you celebrate including each birthday and anniversary!

Sangria Recipes

Regional Sangria Recipes

Every region of the world - and every region of a country - has its own specific take on flavors and customs. This might be easily seen on a grand scale - Chinese food is very different from Mexican food. But even if you go area by area within China you'd be amazed at how much the different regions differ from each other in terms of food types, spices used, sauces, and more.

The same is true with Sangria. At its core, sangria is a mixture of wine, fruit and liqueur. Even just looking at fruits, different locations are very much known for different types of fruits! Hawaii is known for its pineapples. Georgia is known for its peaches. Michigan has world-famous cherries. The list goes on and on. If you were to make a sangria with the best fruit that your specific region is known for, the richness of its flavor would probably far outshine the same sangria made halfway around the world, where they had to truck in frozen versions of your fruit.

The key with regional sangrias is often to enjoy them with matching food! If you make a delicious Italian sangria, mix up a plate of spaghetti and meatballs to eat with it. For a Mexican sangria, how about a burrito or nachos? The more you get the taste sensations to merge in an authentic manner, the more wonderfully the combinations meld!

Sangria Recipes

Summary

Sangria is an incredibly versatile drink which can be anything you want it to be. You can go for sweet and peachy, dark and blueberry, or any flavor combination in between. Because the drinks involve fresh fruits, they can be healthy for you as well.

Start with these recipes as a guideline - then experiment and explore on your own. You could create the best new taste sensation to hit the world since chocolate chips were combined with cookie dough!

Enjoy!

About the Author

Lisa Shea was lucky enough to grow up in a wine loving household. As soon as she reached the legal age, she began to explore the world of wine options. She greatly enjoys visiting wineries and seeing first-hand how vintages are created.

Lisa believes that every type of wine has potential - from cherry wine, to cabernet on Long Island, to sparkling wine in New Mexico. If you keep an open mind and a willing palate, you never know what you might discover!

For more information on wines, visit WineIntro.com

Other Books by Lisa Shea:

Champagne Cocktail Recipes

Low Carb – First Two Weeks
Low Carb Charts
Microwave Low Carb Recipes
Quick No-Cook Low Carb Recipes

Index

Made in the USA
Coppell, TX
27 September 2023

22113843R00085